FOR

BOYS AND GIRLS.

PUBLISHED BY THE
AMERICAN TRACT SOCIETY,
NO. 28 CORNHILL, BOSTON

GEO. C. RAND & AVERY
ELECTROTYPERS AND PRINTERS, 3 CORNHILL, BOSTON.

CONTENTS

Home Stories.

RUTH'S FIRST JOURNEY.

LITTLE Ruth stood at the front window of a large farm-house, and looked eagerly down the village road. Occasionally she glanced with great satisfaction at her crimson merino frock, her holiday attire; for every day this child ran about the farm hunting for eggs, and giving the aid of her little hands wherever they were needed, in a plainer dress of dark stuff, and a long-sleeved, gingham apron. An unusual event was about to take place in Ruth's life. She was going to visit an aunt who lived twenty miles away, and, as the two places were not connected by a railroad, it had been arranged that an old minister, who was returning to the village, should carry with him, in his chaise, the little traveler. This accounted for the agitation Ruth felt, while waiting in her warm coat and straw hat for the coming of the venerable man. Ruth had also under her care a thick shawl and a basket, into which she peeped frequently to see if the red apples and cakes of maple sugar were safe, and on the steps her hair trunk was placed. Now, this journey happened many years ago, when little girls seldom went away from home with their clothes packed in trunks by themselves. All others in the farm-house were eating dinner. Ruth had begged her mother to let her watch for the chaise, meanwhile.

It was that pleasant season of the year when the sap springs again into the trees, and the violets know that it is time to open; when the little straws and threads are picked up by the builders of cunning nests. It was spring, too, in Ruth's life; she was full of happy anticipation. When the old horse first came in sight, Ruth called out joyfully; the family gathered about her, glad to help, in any way, the child who was always willing to help others.

The chaise approached slowly, and at last stopped before the gate. A mild, kind face looked out; Ruth saw the silvery hair and the white cravat, and began to regret her coming ride. One brother took up the hair trunk and strapped it on a rack behind the chaise; the father shook hands with the minister, and lifted Ruth carefully to the seat by his side. Another brother handed the shawl and basket to be stowed away in the vacant space between them, for Ruth was very small. The mother stood in the door-way smiling another good-by; the sisters laughed and talked to cheer poor Ruth, for she had tearful eyes at the prospect of going away so far with this grave old minister.

The reins were gently pulled, and the obedient horse resumed his usual pace; the old chaise creaked and rocked, and Ruth had fairly commenced her long-talked-of journey. She looked timidly at her companion; he was apparently meditating on some subject far beyond her comprehension. Little Ruth felt very much as if she was shut up with an old-fashioned book of divinity. The good man was indeed full of thought; the mysterious providences of God filled his mind, and he pondered on the days of old. He was quite forgetful, for a time, of the child intrusted to his care; she had taken such a very short step in life that he knew not what to say to her; his thoughts and words were "grown up," not adapted to childish ears.

Ruth busied herself with studying the horse and his heavy harness, then the narrow view visible from the chaise. Just as Ruth's tongue was beginning to feel restless, in its unaccustomed stillness, and the road grew very flat and uninteresting, and just as she was wondering whether she had better eat an apple, the old minister remembered that he had in his chaise a little girl, and came down from his solemn thoughts. In vain, he tried to think of something to say to her; perhaps she was sleepy; he turned toward her, but the bright eyes were watching him curiously. When they reached a long hill, where the horse walked in a very moderate way, the old minister made one more effort, and said to Ruth, "Little girl, do you love the Lord Jesus Christ?" Ruth's heart began to beat very fast when she heard this question; she was old enough to know the whole mystery of godliness, and felt afraid that her answer would astonish and displease her companion; at last, after much hesitation. she replied faintly, "Yes; I believe I do."

"Do you?" said the old man, with a smile of joy; "I'm glad! I'm so glad!" then both were silent again. Ruth began to meditate, now, on some of the very things which had been in the mind of her old friend. She was a little frightened at herself for saying so decidedly that she loved the Lord Jesus, for she was not quite sure that she did in reality possess that new heart; but she could not bear to say to this minister of

Christ that she did not love the dear Saviour who had suffered little children to come unto him.

The twenty miles began to seem long to Ruth; she was anxious to reach her aunt's that her attention might be diverted from that haunting question. She sat on the very edge of the seat, that she might the better watch the farm-houses they passed. The sap-pails in the maple-trees, the cows in the yard, made her think of home, and their gathering about the tea-table. The old horse jogged along slower than ever; Ruth wrapped her shawl about her, and nibbled quietly a cake of maple sugar. To her great relief, the scattered houses of the village at length appeared. Nor was it very long before the aunt's familiar face banished from Ruth the tinge of homesickness which the evening lights had inspired. Ruth did not again remember that question until, left alone by her aunt, she knelt to pray her evening prayer. Then the words, "Lovest thou me?" rang in her ears, and her heart could not answer.

Long after this ride had faded entirely from the recollection of the old minister, he was again preaching in the village where Ruth lived one of his last sermons. As he left the pulpit, a young girl lingered in the aisle to speak with him.

"I am that little Ruth," she said, "who rode in your chaise, of whom you asked a question which troubled me until I could answer it aright. Then I did not love the Lord Jesus

Christ; but now I can truly say, 'Thou knowest all things, thou knowest that I love thee.'"

Tears of holy joy filled the old man's eyes. That one question will add to the brightness of his crown, will save a soul from eternal death. That dull and dreary ride was full of blessedness to Ruth, for through eternity she will repeat with ever-growing confidence, "Thou knowest all things, thou *knowest* that I love thee."

THE CHILDREN'S PSALM.

LITTLE did David think, when he wrote "The Lord is my shepherd," how many lambs of the flock, down to the end of the world, would call it "*my psalm;*" how often it would be lisped on mothers' knees when the daylight was fading; how bright eyes would grow still brighter when the minister in the pulpit chanced to read it from the big church Bible; how it would be loved and cherished through life, above all the other songs of the sweet singer of Israel, till the little one, grown old and gray-headed, standing in the gathering shadows of the dark valley, could still say, "I will fear no evil, for thou art with me!"

The dearest lamb to me in all the flock was sitting on my

knee in the Sabbath twilight, repeating the psalm with many a gallant dash at the long, hard words, and sinking back with a sigh of self-congratulation when the last verse was reached. For a few minutes he leaned his head on my shoulder, and silently watched the stars as they came out one after another in the darkening sky,— but silence was not a frequent guest on those prattling lips.

"Auntie," he said, "where is the house of the Lord? did you ever go there?"

So I told him, in words he could understand, of the house not made with hands,—the place Jesus has gone to prepare,— the beautiful city whose streets are of gold, and its gates of pearl, and of the multitude of little children who are there, with their music and gladness, their tears all wiped away, and their pain gone for ever.

"And are there green pastures there, and still waters?" he asked with sparkling eyes. I turned to the twenty-second chapter of Revelation, and read a few verses about the river, clear as crystal, and the tree of life on either side.

"And is mamma there? and when they packed little Alice up in a box, did they send her to the house of the Lord for ever?"

"Yes, mamma is there, and baby Alice is there, too; but it was only her little body that we put in the coffin,— the angels came for her soul, and carried it right to Jesus' home."

"Let us go there, auntie,—such a nice place to live in!"

"We can't go there, dear, till God sends for us."

"Well, if an angel *should* come some afternoon, and say God had sent him for little Eddie Arnold, you would let me go with him, wouldn't you?"

"Yes, darling," I said; "I couldn't keep little Eddie, if Jesus wanted him;" but in my heart I prayed that the day might be far distant when the boy should be wanted among the angels.

A few weeks had passed. The rose-bushes that were then showing their first green leaves were now full of blossoms,—the Sabbath twilight was again settling over the earth; but the Angel of Death had come for the little lamb I loved,—he was leading him even then into the valley.

All through the day he had lain in a stupor, but now his eyes opened, and, as they met mine, he said, "Say it, auntie,—my psalm."

Slowly I repeated, "The Lord is my shepherd; I shall not want. He maketh me to lie down in green pastures: he leadeth me beside the still waters."

Dreamily he repeated after me,—"green pastures,—still waters."

Ah, my darling! the waters were *very* "still" for you,—still and low, scarcely wetting the little feet that passed through them so fearlessly. One gasp, and there was another lamb safe in the fold of the Good Shepherd.

THE LITTLE SLAVE.

I DWELL where the sun
  Shines gayly and bright,
Where flowers of rich beauty
  Are ever in sight;

Here blooms the magnolia,
  Here orange-trees wave;
But oh, not for *me*,—
  I'm a poor little slave!

They say, "Sunny South"
  Is the name of my home;
'Tis here that your robins
  And bluebirds are come,
While snows cover nests up,
  And angry winds rave;
They may rest here,—not *I*;
  I'm a poor little slave!

Here beautiful mothers,
  'Mid splendors untold,
Their fairy-like babes
  To their fond bosoms fold;
My mamma's worked out,
  And lies here in the grave;
There's none to kiss *me*,—
  I'm a poor little slave!

I've heard mistress telling
  Her sweet little son,
What Jesus, the loving,
  For children has done;

Perhaps little black ones
He also will save;
I ask him to take *me*,
A poor little slave!

ONE MORE WORKER.

MATTIE had been very sick, but her life was spared. There was more work for her to do. Her pale, thin face was a perpetual reminder to Willis of God's great mercy in giving her back to them after taking her down so near to the shadow of the grave. He was almost constantly with her, beguiling the tedious hours of convalescence with stories or quiet talk. When she slept, he held the little blue-veined hand, or softly smoothed the brown hair. "The boys" might have laughed, had they seen him; but what were the "boys" to him, compared with Mattie? Their laugh was not the bugbear that it had been. He seemed changed in more ways than one.

One evening while Mattie slept, Willis sat with his mother in the parlor. The lamps had not been lighted, and the coal-fire but faintly illumined the room. Mrs. Walker smoothed back the hair from her boy's forehead, musingly. "Well, Willis," said she at length, "where are you?"

"A good way off, mother; among the stars."

"Rather a long journey, Willis, for one evening!"

"Yes'm; I know it; I was thinking"—

"Thinking what?"

"I was thinking how every thing in nature is useful, and has something to do; and I wondered if stars have any thing to do. Have they?"

"You know what the sun is to us, and the moon; and think what the North Star is to the traveler and the sailor; and then to the poor slaves it is a kind of star of Bethlehem, guiding to the land where for them Liberty lies new-born."

"Yes, mother."

"Perhaps some of these stars are North Stars to other worlds; perhaps some are suns and moons. Every star has its own part in the wonderful economy of the Universe."

"Well," said Willis, presently, "to come down a little, what do you suppose is *my* work?"

"Can't you possibly find out?"

"Why, I don't see any *regular* work;—there's enough small fry to see to; but I've been looking ahead!"

Mrs. Walker smiled. "The large work will appear in time. You know the saying: There's a loom for every man who can weave. See to your 'small fry' carefully, and if you really want to be a worker, God will provide work."

Willis spoke earnestly, "I do want to be a worker, mother.

I never used to think much about it; but lately it has seemed to me I ought to be doing something."

"Why, dear Willis?"

"Not because Mattie is better," said Willis in a choked voice; "but I've thought up a great many things. I don't deserve such mercy at all, and if God loves me so, I want to love him and do something for him. I mean, any way, I want to stand up *on his side.* It all came over me by degrees, how selfish I had been,—always trying to make *number one* comfortable, and forgetting other people. I know it wasn't Christ's way, and I'm determined it shan't be mine."

"That is right, Willis," said his mother. "If you bravely and earnestly try to follow Christ, he himself will help you. There is strong help to be had simply for the asking."

"What do you think my work is, mother?" said Willis. "I must take care of my feelings, and"——

"No, my son; leave that to Christ. *That* is not part of your work."

"Well, I mean I've got to do right, and that's hard enough; but I want something else. I feel as if I could dig right through a mountain!"

Mrs. Walker smiled, but the smile grew sad.

"'Doing right' covers a great deal of ground, my boy! Your mountain is yourself. The better you know Willis Walker, the clearer you will see that you have plenty of work on hand! The 'great work' will come along in due time. You must be faithful, upright, true, in every little thing. You can honor Christ in your every-day life, at school, at home, at play. You can live such a beautiful, holy life, now while you are only a school-boy, that it will help the Saviour's cause."

"I hope I shall, mother. But if I happen to forget? If I torment Mattie before I think?"

"Then you will ask forgiveness of One who will be more grieved than she; and if you are in earnest, you will be willing to ask *her* forgiveness, too."

Willis winced as he thought how his pride must be brought down before he could do that. "Any way, you rebel," said he to himself, as he went up-stairs, "you and I will have some tussles, I guess, and you don't beat either! with God's help," he added, reverently.

"Mattie, you awake?"

"Yes, Willis."

"If you'll guess this riddle, I'll roast the best sweet apple in the house for your supper!"

"Oh, dear!" said Mattie; "I'll try, but I know I can't guess."

"What enemy is there, who hates boys, who torments them from morning till night, who helps them do wrong and keeps them from confessing it, who attacks them on all sides like a swarm of bees? Sometimes he kills the boy, and sometimes the boy kills him (as I intend to); but the strangest thing is, nobody ever saw this enemy. Now show the Yankee colors, little Mattie!"

A SCENE AT A RAILROAD STATION.

Among the green hills of New Hampshire, where the flowers bloom wild, and the bright berries grow by the road-side, I was waiting for the cars to take me to my home, when I heard a loud whistle, and rumbling and rattling through the woods they came; but instead of the nice cars, with open windows, came a long train of boards and barrels, and huge boxes, holding I don't know what; then one car all closed up save the sides, where there were long slats put across. And what do you think I could see behind them? Just as many sheep and lambs as could be put in; and as the cars stopped a moment, there they stood, looking through the narrow windows, no doubt wishing they could get out to nibble the sweet clover, and lie under the shady trees,—for they looked so hot and crowded and dusty I know they would have enjoyed it very much.

Little boys and girls sometimes like to ride in the cars, for they have nice seats and plenty of room to make themselves comfortable; but I don't believe the poor sheep and lambs *ever* like to ride in such a way; and I could not help thinking how patient they were, how gentle and quiet, although they were leaving the bright green fields and sweet clover, and were shut up so close, where they could not even rest themselves by lying down.

Don't you remember that Jesus was called the Lamb of God? This was because he was so gentle and good; and don't you think we all ought to be like him? But we very often forget and grow impatient and fretful; but I hope that when we are tempted to be so, we may remember the Lamb of God and try very hard to please him.

God, who made the sheep and lambs, takes care of them, as well as of the little sparrows. Let us love him, and ask him to take care of us, also, and take us when we die to the fold of the great Shepherd above.

JESSIE'S HYACINTH.

"Oh, I do wish I was grown up!" exclaimed Jessie Burns one morning as she looked out of the window. It was no uncommon wish with her, nor is it with other little girls eight years old; but her tone indicated some new reason for it just then; so her mother asked, "Why, my child?"

"Because I want to be of some use in the world. I mean to be ever so good, mamma, when I am grown up, and to do good, oh, *so much* good,—more than any body ever did before,—don't you hope I shall?"

"Yes, dear, I hope you will do a great deal."

"I don't know but I shall be a missionary: I've been thinking that would be a good way, wouldn't it, mamma?"

"Yes, a very good way, if you were fitted for one, and the way should be opened for you."

"I guess I'll go to Africa; Mr. Lindley told us such nice stories about Africa, you know; only they are all black folks there, real jet-black negroes; I shouldn't much like to live with black folks all the time. But then a missionary wouldn't mind such things."

"No, and you wouldn't go to have a nice time, but to do good."

"Yes; and I should like to see ostriches and antelopes, and all such curious things. I could, you know," she added, seeing a smile hovering about her mother's lips, "while I was doing good."

"Yes."

"And oh, I hope we should have to live in wagons, as they did ever so many weeks, and be drawn about by oxen. Did you hear him tell how they used to tie the oxen to the wagon at night, and how when they were all laid down in the wagon and most asleep, they could hear them breathing outside, and hear the lions roar off in the great woods close by?"

The mother thought of a little girl she knew, who screamed with fear, if only a little mouse nibbled at the wall. Perhaps Jessie did, too, for after a little meditation, she said,—

"I guess missionaries are never afraid of any thing; and he said they didn't come near them, because they built a bright fire to keep them off."

Jessie ran on at much greater length, planning the details of her wandering African life, ending at last with a great sigh, and the exclamation with which she began, "Oh, if I were only grown up,—I can't go till I am!"

"Not to Africa, Jessie, but you can begin to do good now, and that will be the best way of preparing yourself to become a missionary."

"Why, how can I do good, mamma? I can't think of any way."

"You know Miss Dana, and how long she has been sick, and how very fond she is of flowers?"

"Yes, mamma," said Jessie, greatly wondering what that could have to do with her question.

"I was thinking of her this morning, and wishing I could do something for her, she is so lonely and often sad; and just then, my eye fell on your beautiful hyacinth, and I thought how much she would enjoy it."

"But you don't mean that I should give *that* away!"

"You could, if you wished to do good."

"Why, mamma, I love that better than all my flowers,—a great deal better!" and her eyes filled with tears.

"But you can never do good, my child, or have a genuine desire to, without being willing to make sacrifices. Self-denial is the very essence of benevolence,—its life, without which it can never attain to strength or value."

The struggle began in little Jessie's heart,—that struggle so often going on in young hearts and old, between inclination and conscience. She felt as if she ought to be self-denying, but she did not want to be; and it really cost her a severe effort to decide to carry her cherished plant to cheer the lonely invalid. But once decided, her heart felt lighter; and after dinner, she tripped over to Miss Dana's with the hyacinth in her hand, her cheeks glowing and eyes sparkling with a consciousness that she was doing good.

"Oh, mamma!" she exclaimed, on her return, "Miss Dana was so glad and so pleased, she could hardly keep from crying.

She said the very sight of the beautiful blossoms sent sad thoughts out of her mind, and made her feel better than she had for weeks. I am so glad I carried it to her; it made her happy, and me happy, too."

And the glad mother folded her own sweet flower in her arms lovingly, and gave her a tender kiss. *Her* heart was happy too.

DON'T SMOKE.

Oh, little boy, don't smoke, now don't! It is a dreadful habit. It will ruin your health, waste your money, disgrace your parents, and make you disagreeable to every person of refinement or decency. You say it is manly. What makes you think so? Because men do it? But men steal and swear and drink rum. And are these practices manly, and are you going to imitate these, too? Oh, no, you are mistaken; it is not manly. I'll tell you why. It is not manly to do any thing wrong. It is mean to do wrong.

Is it manly to make yourself sick? "Oh," you say, "smoking doesn't make me sick." But it did once, before you got used to the taste and smell of the nasty weed. I recollect very well that summer morning, when you came in from your play in such a hurry, and threw yourself down on the lounge in the basement, looking as white as a sheet. How faint and death-like you felt! You were frightened, too, and so was your poor mother. "Dear me," she exclaimed, "what can be the matter with Henry? Why, he was just as well as ever at breakfast time! Why, Henry, what ails you? What has happened?" But you never answered a word, and only tossed your head from side to side, growing more pale and sick every moment. "Run for the doctor this moment, Bridget, and go in for Aunt Carrie, too. Henry is so sick, I don't know but he'll die."

How did that word "die" make you feel just then? Did it make you feel any easier in body or mind? Then Aunt Carrie came in, and what did she say? She didn't seem so very much alarmed after she had stood and looked at you a moment. But you saw her smile a queer sort of a smile as she turned around to your mother, and said, "He'll be better by and by, Mary; don't be worried. It's nothing but that cigar I saw him smoking this morning."

"A cigar? This morning? My Henry smoking? Why, Carrie, what do you mean?"

"Henry knows well enough what I mean," said Aunt Carrie; and she turned again and fixed her large black eyes full on you. How red you grew all at once!—and you threw your head round with a quick motion as if you were very sick again, and tried to cover up your blushing face. But it had told the truth.

Well, your mother wasn't quite so much frightened after that, but she had a heavy, aching feeling away down in her heart, that was very hard to bear. "Oh, dear!" she kept saying to herself, "Oh, dear!" And when the doctor came and gave you that ugly emetic that was so hard to take, and made you feel so badly after you had swallowed it, your mother didn't feel half so much concerned at your pain, as she did at the thought of what you had done, and she hoped that the nauseous medicine would for ever cure you. You remember how she talked to you afterward, don't you? Yes; you will never forget that. I am sure you think of it every time you put a cigar into your mouth. What a pity!

Is it manly to waste your money, or your father's money, to buy cigars with? No indeed! the money belongs to God, and it is wicked to use it for what can do you no good, and still worse to spend it for what will do you harm. If all the money spent for cigars was put together in one great pile, how much there would be, and how much good could be accomplished with it. I know some men that have smoked their money almost all away. Wouldn't you rather have gold than smoke for your portion? I would.

And do you think it is manly to make yourself disagreeable to nice people? I can't bear to go any where near a person that smokes. I know a great many others who feel just the same. I wouldn't marry a man who smoked, — not I. I couldn't love him at all, he would be so disgusting to me. You had better take care, little boy. Perhaps you may take a great fancy to somebody, one of these days, who feels just as I do, and it might hurt your feelings very much for you to find out that she didn't like you and the reason why.

Oh, little boy, don't smoke! Throw away that cigar, and promise yourself and God that you will never touch your lips to another as long as you live.

LUCY LEE.

A DEAR lover of all that is beautiful in nature is little Lucy Lee. A gleam of sunlight is herself, wherever she goes; up-stairs in the nursery, or in the playroom, down in the kitchen, out in the garden among the flowers, in the woods and fields looking for the first blue violets, or sitting quietly in her mother's room with her sewing, as you see her here, she seems the same happy child, such as makes older hearts grow light, and sad faces glad.

Perhaps one reason why Lucy always seems so happy is, that her mother never looks cross, and she has been taught from infancy that nothing is worth a cross look or an angry word.

Not that Lucy never does wrong. I do not think she means to be naughty,—for if she is, one sight of her mother's grieved face will almost break her heart, and she is not satisfied until her mother's kiss, and a promise that she "will not feel badly any more," tells her she is forgiven,—but she always seems so happy, I feel she can not be often naughty.

She has had her ramble out of doors, and has finished her lessons with mamma, and now the little fingers are busily stitching a garment for Dolly, whose summer wardrobe is "all out of order," Lucy says, having been very much diminished by the gifts she has sent from it to other dolls, not so well provided for. She has climbed up into the window where she loves to sit, not forgetting the hyacinth which she carries with her from room to room, that she may lose nothing of its sweetness; and busy you see her as any young mother who is aroused to the wants of her little family by the soft, faint-away air of the coming spring.

"Oh, mamma, do see this dear little robin so close to the

window! I do believe it is the very one that built his nest here last year, and he has come back to see if it is ready for him. Do you remember how Jamie used to watch him picking up straws, and sometimes the threads and bits of cotton we threw out for him? Oh, I am so glad spring has come!" and then without awaiting any reply, she went on thinking aloud. "How Jamie would love to see them now! He used to say 'birdie' so cunningly, and listen for their singing, and make his hands go so fast, laughing to see how quickly he could make them fly away. Oh, I do wish he was here now, mamma! Do you think there are birds in heaven?"

Her mother was silent; and in a moment Lucy dropped her work, and, jumping down from the window, she clasped her mother lovingly as she saw her tearful eyes, saying, "I am very sorry I said so, I didn't mean to make you cry, but I only thought how Jamie used to love the birds. That was not wrong, was it, mamma?"

"Oh, no! my daughter, but you brought him so before me as I used to see him standing and begging to get up to the window; and then I felt how we had missed him."

"'P'ease, sister, p'ease,' he used to say, and stamp his little feet as if he could not wait a minute. *Don't* you wish he was here?" she added, earnestly.

"No, Lucy, I can not say that, for he is where he will never be sick any more, nor tired."

"But, mamma, won't he be very lonely away from you? He was always shy of strangers, and there is no one in heaven who knows Jamie."

"Oh, yes! dear grandma is there, and Aunt Martha, and there are many little children there too, and Jesus, who loves Jamie better even than we could, and there is music there."

"And Jamie loved music. I used to think I should never want to go to heaven without you and papa, but now he is there it seems more home-like, and not so far off."

"That is one reason why Jesus took Jamie to himself, I suppose, to make us think more of heaven."

Lucy sat thinking.—"Do you suppose I should go to heaven?" she said, in a tremulous voice. "You have often told me, none but good people could go there, and I know I am not always good, for I sometimes make you sorry; but I am so glad I was kind to Jamie! I don't believe I ever hurt him."

"No, Lucy, I don't think you ever did, and that will always be pleasant for you to remember, but that would not take you to heaven. If you were ever so good, you could not go there, unless Jesus had come to this world and died for you."

"Is that why I always say, 'for Jesus' sake,' when I ask God for any thing?"

"Yes; we could none of us go to heaven, if it were not for what Jesus has done for us. You are too young yet to understand how it is, but you can remember that he is your best friend, and thank him for opening for us the way to such a happy home."

"I'm sure I ought to love him very much and do something for him. Could I, mamma?"

"Yes, Lucy; you can do what he most wants you to do. You can give him yourself, and that means to give him your love and your service, to live to please him, instead of pleasing yourself; and he will help you to do this."

Lucy went to her room with a softened heart, and prayed more earnestly than ever before, that Jesus would take her for one of his loving, little friends, and make her very good and very useful.

Dear little reader, will you not do so too?

A GOOD ANSWER.

A YOUNG lady in a Sabbath school, a few mornings since, asked her class how soon a child should give its heart to God. One little girl said, When thirteen years old; another, ten; another, six. At length the last spoke: "Just as soon as we know who God is." Could there be a better reply?

MOTIVES AND ACTIONS.

"THERE is one thing Miss Leighton always has in her prayer, mother, that I don't exactly understand."

"What is it Bell?" asked her mother, gently, as she noticed Bell's hesitation.

"Something about our motives, mother; she asks that 'we may be careful that our actions shall be the result of pure motives.' And I am sure she thinks a great deal about that, from something I heard her say to-day. It was when Bessie Green came in at recess, and asked permission to go with a poor woman who was lame and carrying a basket of work, and help her by taking the basket for her to her home. It was a long way up the hill, and Bessie did not get back until the school was nearly closed."

"What was it that Miss Leighton said?"

"One of the older girls asked her, just after Bessie started, 'if that was not beautiful in Bess?' and Miss Leighton said, 'It is always pleasant to see persons kind to the unfortunate, but the beauty and worth of the action depend upon the motive.' There was a curious little smile, too, about the corners of her mouth which made me think she meant something special about Bess."

"*Perhaps* not. Could *you* think of any other reason Bessie might have had for asking to go, besides helping the lame woman?"

"To be tnought well of by the other girls, do you mean?"

"That *might* have been the reason,—could you think of another?"

A little pink tinge covered Bell's cheeks as she replied, "If *I* had asked to go with the lame woman, there might have been another."

"What, Bell?"

I should have been away from my arithmetic recitation, and sometimes I might have liked that, but to-day I shouldn't, for I had my lesson perfectly, and had all my examples ready on my slate."

"I can show you what your teacher means by being careful of our motives, Bell. Suppose you had not had your lesson, and had asked to help the poor woman. The act would have appeared the same, but the motive—a desire to cover your own fault by apparent kindness to another—would not have been worthy of the action. Bessie may not have thought of her lesson, and only have had the best motive. But, while it is not right for us to judge others too severely, we should scan our own acts carefully. We shall never gain any thing but shame and confusion in the end from acts, however noble or praiseworthy they may appear, if He who reads our hearts, and sees the first springs of action there, is not pleased with the motives from which they spring.

"Suppose a little girl was often giving her mother trouble by staying one or two hours longer than she had permission, when allowed to visit little friends. Suppose, one day, she was told to be at home precisely at three, and, just as she was starting from the door, overheard her mother say to the servant, 'We shall ride at three this afternoon,' do you think, if that little girl was home just a little before three that day, that she would deserve particular commendation for being obedient?"

Again the little pink flush came, and Bell said, as she remembered her own fault, "Mother, I see there is some one who watches motives besides Miss Leighton."

Bell's mother smiled, as she replied, "If we take good care of them, Bell, it will only be a pleasant thought that others sometimes read them; and could we live so as to be *glad* that one perfectly good Being always knows them, and loves to approve them when right, we should be happy indeed."

HOW PICTURES ARE MADE.

Many a little reader while looking at the beautiful pictures in this book, has said, "I wonder how these pictures are made!" We will try to describe the process.

In the first place, the artist procures a piece of wood, of the exact size of the picture he is to make. This is generally boxwood,—a kind which has a very fine grain, and grows compact and hard. This is sawed *across the grain,* in blocks about an inch long, which will of course be as large as the stick was from which they were sawed. As this, however, is rarely more than six or eight inches in diameter, two or more blocks are joined together when a large picture is to be engraved.

When the block is shaped and smoothed, its surface is whitened, and it is then ready for use. Next the designer draws upon it the picture, in pencil. Then the engraver cuts it in the block, using a tool called a *graver*, — a sort of triangular-shaped chisel, which is pushed along in the wood, as shown in our cut above. A rod supports a magnifying glass near the eye of the artist, to enable him to make the delicate lines with the utmost care and nicety.

When the work is done, the picture will show on the block cut *in relief*. That is, the lines and points are left *above* the surface, while all the spaces which are to appear white are cut away. For example, in this outline figure of a dog, every thing is cut out but the bare outline itself. This, standing higher than the other parts, will receive the ink, when the cut is to be printed, and leave it upon the paper which is pressed upon it. Otherwise, if the outline itself were cut out, it would appear thus: —

The engraved block, when finished, is then set up with the type, ready for printing.

The beauty of the picture, it is obvious, will depend mostly on the skill of the designer and engraver. These are generally different persons, the two arts, indeed, being reckoned as entirely distinct from each other. The designer commonly puts his name on one corner of the picture, with the letters "del." for "*delinivit*," *i. e.* "designed;" the engraver on another corner, with "sc." for "*sculpsit*," *i. e.* "engraved." Often, however, the names alone are regarded as sufficient.

Of course these engravings must be expensive. Several days, and sometimes weeks, are required to complete a large picture. So much, however, do they add to the beauty and interest of books and papers, that they are now very extensively used. Most people are willing to pay enough more for handsomely illustrated publications to make up the difference in cost.

LITTLE MAY AND THE OLD MAN.

One sunny day, fair little May
  Went through the woodland near;
Tripping along by brook and stone,
  Without a thought of fear;
Though she had never known the way
Until she found it out that day.

Outside the wood, a path she took,
  That to the meadow led;
And there she saw, with book in hand,
  A man with hoary head;

His smile was sweet, his eyes were blue;
He said, "Young lady, whence come you?"

"I'm little May; from home I came
To take a summer walk;
May I sit down upon the bank?
I'd like with you to talk.
What is that book within your hand?
Can I its meaning understand?"

"Sweet lady, 'tis a blessed book,
Which makes my old eyes see,
In that calm sky which hangs above,
A blessed company.
Three children have I living there,
And I expect their home to share."

Said little May with wondering eyes,
"And will it show to me,
Oh, good old man, as well as you,
That glorious company?"
"Dear lady, yes; each human eye
Their heavenly beauty may descry.

"Please read your book here by the brook."
And so the old man read
Sweet words that filled her with surprise,
Until she softly said,

"I did not know there is a place
Where we can see a Saviour's face."

"He came to earth," the old man said,
"To die for you and me."
"Why did he die?" "That we might join
That glorious company."
And still the old man read his book,
And still sung on the chiming brook.

He read how Jesus put his arms
Around each little child;
And how, with hands upon its head,
In holy words and mild,
Each tender little form He blessed,
Then laid it on the mother's breast.

And little May, full many a day,
Passed through the woodland lone,
And always found the good old man
Upon his mossy stone;
And by the little singing brook,
He read from his delightful book.

WHAT SUSY SAID.

Susy's tongue runs as fast as any little girl's can, about a great many things; but there is nothing she loves better to talk about than what her brother Sammy can do, — how he carries her on his sled, how well he skates, how strong he is, and how kind.

One evening, Susy went to a little prayer-meeting. Something was said to the children there. They were told that now is the time for them to come to Christ; that, as they could not be happy if their mothers were angry with them, no more could they be happy while God is angry with them; that to love God *now* with all their hearts is the only way to be happy now, as well as to escape the wrath of God for ever, and be happy with him eternally.

Susy said afterwards to a lady who was at the meeting, "Why, I never felt so before. I thought what Mr. C. said meant something. And when I looked at you, and saw the tears on your face, I thought you thought it meant something. And when Mr. G. began to pray for us, that we might not grieve that kind Saviour, who said, 'Suffer the little ones to come unto me,' and who died for us, I was sure he thought it meant something too, and that it was time to give myself to Christ. And I have been trying; but it is hard work to come alone, and I am afraid I shall not stick to it. I want my brothers to be Christians; but I think if Sammy will, he would help me most, for he would stick to it."

So Susy tried to think how she could persuade Sammy to come with her and help her in this new way on which she had set out.

She could not attend the evening meetings, unless one of her brothers would go with her, and Sammy used to wonder at first why she was so anxious to go, and sometimes tried to persuade her to stay at home; but he loved so well to please her that her pleadings usually prevailed.

She had begun that very night to read a chapter in the Bible every evening, but she often found verses which she could not understand. She had been so accustomed to go to him for an explanation of whatever puzzled her, that it was very natural to ask him about these. He could not tell her any thing about one of them, when she first asked him, but after a while he came back and said,—

"Oh, I remember, now, what my Sabbath-school teacher said about that."

How happy that teacher was to hear that one who had often pained her by appearing very inattentive in the class, had laid up in his memory some of the things she had tried to teach him years before; more happy still, when she learned that he had begun to read the Bible with his sister, and when, a few days later, he took hold of her hand, and, with eyes full of tears, said,—

"I want to thank you a thousand times for the book you gave me so long ago, 'Come to Jesus.' I've been reading it lately, and I hope it has done me good."

Will you not pray that Susy and Sammy may both "stick to it;" and will *you* not begin to "cleave unto the Lord"?

HOW GOD TAKES CARE OF HIS CHILDREN.

In my walks across Boston Common a year ago, I often met a little lame girl, whose interesting countenance and quiet manner, as she offered her candy for sale, attracted my attention. Sometimes, I bought a trifle to encourage her; at others, gave her a penny. She told me that her family were very poor, and she tried to help them all she could. One of her little brothers was also lame; both were obliged to use crutches.

When the cold weather came on, the little girl was missing from her accustomed place; but, as soon as the warm breath of returning Spring covered the trees with verdure, and the ground with its rich, living carpet of green, she returned and offered her small stock of candy to the passer-by as before.

One day, in July last, I found the mother with her little

girl. She had a care-worn, anxious countenance, just one of those we can not forget; while tottering about, now on this side, then on that, was a baby, who seemed to have just become conscious that it could walk alone. It was rather pretty, and its dress, though poor and worn, was neat and clean. Such little ones always attract me; they remind me of the dear ones whose playful, winning ways once made up much of the happiness of our household, and do still, though their home is now a heavenly one. Taking a penny from my purse, I gave it to the baby, and, nodding to the mother, who seemed pleased at the notice, I passed on.

Upon reaching home, a half-dollar, which had been given to me for a particular use, was missing. Where could it be? I recollected a recent purchase I had made, and was certain that it was then in my purse. I had opened the purse but once afterwards, when I took from it the penny. Could I have dropped it at that time? I thought not. "Well, wherever it is, I hope it may do somebody some good," thought I, and it passed from my mind.

Two months later, I found the mother and her little girl at the old place; a small table stood near, on which were temptingly spread out apples, candy, etc. As I approached, the little girl ran out to meet me, and the mother exclaimed, "Oh, dear lady! I bless God that I see you, and thank you for the help that you gave me that day in my great trouble."

"When was it?" said I.

"The day that you gave my baby the penny and *half-dollar*. I have prayed to the blessed Jesus for you every day since."

"I am very glad that it helped you, but I *dropped* it," said I.

"Yes," she replied, "when you gave it to the baby," seeming not to understand me. "Oh, that was the day of my great want. My children had nothing to eat, and my oldest girl lay on the floor crying with hunger. That was dreadful,—that day of my *very* great want!" she repeated. "The money kept my poor children from starving, and if it had not been for that, I never could have got this table. I do not sell very much, but we have never been so badly off as then."

"This was the way then," said I to myself, "that my half-dollar went. God wanted it to supply the need of his poor, suffering ones." I was made the instrument of relieving them, and they had prayed that blessings might descend upon me. But it was no act of mine. It was not my intention to bestow the half-dollar upon them; it had been done by a higher power. Could I doubt that it was the hand of a kind, heavenly Father, whose watchful care is extended to all? It was one of those beautiful providences, often unseen and unnoticed by us, of which the world is so full, by which he accomplishes his purposes of mercy and love to his children. The cries of that suffering family had reached his ear, and in infinite wisdom he came to their relief.

THE SUMMER CLOUD, AND ITS LESSON.

It had been a day of much unhappiness to my spirit. I had yielded to temptation once, and several times spoken bitterly and hastily to dear friends. When I retired to my room at night, I was so unhappy, that it was long before I could bring myself to pray; but when I had done so, earnestly and repentantly, I was greatly relieved, and soon after my head was laid upon my pillow, I fell asleep. A kind Father watched over me when I could not take any care of myself; and although I had disobeyed and forgotten him during the day, he refreshed me with quiet sleep, and kept evil from me.

At early day I awoke, and to him who should ever receive our first thoughts I offered my morning prayer. One by one, the stars faded away, and a broad beam of light flooded the distant hill-tops; it spread wider and wider, till the sunbeams streamed up the eastern sky. The clouds, which had gathered in one dark mass during the night, now began to separate and move away, hastened by the northerly wind which closely followed in their track.

I had closed my eyes for a few moments, when upon opening them I saw the outline of a hand pointing with one finger toward the rising sun. Instead of passing off as the other clouds had done, it remained stationary for a while, and then gradually faded away, leaving the clear blue sky in its place.

It was a pleasant thought to me that perhaps it was designed that my sometimes doubting, rebellious heart should receive a lesson from this little cloud-hand; for it reminded me of that which is *unseen*, yet ever present, which the believer trusts is conducting him to his heavenly home; leading us through the mazes of this perplexing life to that world where we shall know as we are known, and trouble and sin find no entrance.

The finger of that summer cloud pointed to the glorious sun as he rose to give light to the whole world. It repeated to me the oft-told advice of pastor and Sabbath-school teacher, to look to the Sun of Righteousness, if in darkness or error, that healing and purifying balm might be shed upon my soul by his heavenly beams.

From this hour, dear young reader, let us strive to walk as "children of the light," that when the shadows of death settle over us we may behold "light beyond," and find a happy entrance where there is no night. Then shall we bless and praise the hand which now mixes for us the bitter cup of sorrow or disappointment, feeling that it was good that we were chastened on earth, else perhaps the glories of the upper temple would not have been prepared for us.

LAMBS AT PLAY.

Lambs at play! A whole family! A *happy* family! Was ever any thing more beautiful to see! They are so glad to escape from their winter quarters and enjoy the fresh, tender grass! Those three in the foreground have had such a frolic, playing "hide and go seek" among the low shrubs; or "catch" upon the velvety lawn; and now they are all ready for a jump! Can you not almost hear them say, "One to begin!"

just as you do when you jump on the stout, fresh hay in grandmother's barn?

They seem full of life and frolic, and yet they are not rude. How very soft their touch as they push each other about! You see as they stand here, Bunch does not crowd Bess off one side of the rock, and Bess don't pull Jenny's wool, nor bite her ear, nor step on her toes! Very loving are they in their plays, and so their plays always end happily; and when the mother sheep says "B-a-a," Bess pricks up her ears and says "M-a-a," and scampers off, as fast as her nimble legs can carry her. Bunch and Jenny follow, expecting a call every minute, and obeying even before they hear the voice!

Very beautiful are they, and do you not think it would be very pleasant if every family of brothers and sisters would live together as happily as the lambs seem to?

You need not always be at play as the lambs are just now, to be happy. Play does not always make children happy. Indeed, too much play, or playing with a selfish spirit, makes them very *un*happy, tired, and cross. It is the heart that makes us happy. If that is right, every thing we do is pleasant. If that is wrong, even play is dull and tiresome.

"OUT OF THE MOUTH OF BABES."

'Tis from the little ones, O God,
  Their simple hearts and artless ways,—
Wiser, because more pure than we,
  Thou hast perfected praise.

A tiny creature, scarcely learned
  In words to tell her infant thought,
A nursling of three tender springs,
  This precious lesson taught.

She was abroad where social cheer
  To every friendly lip was pressed,
And love had dainties well prepared
  To please the little guest.

Her father's faith for daily bread
  A daily blessing had implored,
And prayer she deemed with each repast
  Must rise above the board.

And wonderingly she sat, and sad,
  Untasted all the bounty given,—
The master did not pause to thank
  The Giver up in heaven.

Then sorrowful to him she turned,
  And softly lisped, "Pease, sir, pease pay."
Unnoticed or unknown it passed,—
  That sweet request to pray.

And so she bowed her head, and laid
  Her folded hands with reverent care,
And in her baby accents said
  Her little evening prayer.

The guests were silent: she who spoke
  In pure simplicity had prayed;
An aged voice the silence broke,
  As reverently it said,—

"Out of the mouth of babes, O Lord,
  And sucklings" (wondrous are the ways
And wise the counsels of his word)
  "Thou hast perfected praise!"

MY VISIT TO THE DOGS OF ST. BERNARD; OR, KINDNESS BRINGS KINDNESS.

We may often learn from the brutes that surround us lessons of kindness, as well as of wisdom.

When I was a very little girl, not more than six or seven years old perhaps, I received as a birthday present two volumes prettily bound in red morocco. I had often admired them long before they were mine; for, each time that I entered my father's study, I could see them on the shelf, where amongst many others for which I did not care a bit, they seemed to wink out their brilliant and attractive color to me. How perfectly happy I was on a lovely spring morn, when these same coveted treasures were given to me! Yes, they were mine. I had a right to take them, and open them, and even hide them away in my little room, if I chose. For my name was written on the fly-leaf, and no one could dispossess me of them. But, what was the story which those pretty red books told? It was not one only, but a great many, and each one of them was about dogs; — not ill-tempered, ugly, or cross dogs, of course, but intelligent, well-behaved, and kind dogs. These stories were intended to show how even animals can be taught to understand obedience, to feel gratitude, and to return kindness; and no child could read them without making the resolution never to be guilty of the least cruelty, or even the least neglect toward the brave creatures who so often display traits of touching heroism.

I once went to the top of Mount St. Bernard, that lofty pass of the Alps which is occupied by a hospital, celebrated for the kindness of its monks, and of its noble dogs, toward poor travelers who have fallen beneath the terrible snow-storms which sweep through those desolate solitudes. And there I saw a great many of the famous St. Bernard dogs. They originally came from Spain; and yet, now, they would perish if they were carried to a warm climate, for they love snow. These St. Bernard dogs are a brave, courageous race, which God seems to have created to be the friend as well as the companion of man in those dangerous places. No one can look at them without a feeling of great interest, for they share,—consciously, one would think,—the constant perils in which, to save the lives of others, the good monks often risk their own. Some travelers have tried to buy these dogs, but no money could purchase them. One of the monks told me that an Englishman had offered a large sum of money for a fine St. Bernard dog, but he replied to him that the French soldiers had been before him, and were soon made to know that the monks and their dogs could not part. Without them, the generous and Christian charity of these monks would be useless, as it is the dogs, which, obeying their mysterious instinct, go into the mountains and search the deep snow-drifts, where a man, woman, or child, may be buried alive.

The St. Bernard dogs are taken care of with a sort of respectful tenderness, and I felt proud myself to stroke the head of the oldest one, called *Barry*, in honor of one of his ancestors, who immortalized himself in saving the lives of fifteen persons. Barry the first is now "stuffed," and can be seen in the museum at Berne. Around his neck is a little board on which is written a memoir of his services to humanity. What a noble monument to old Barry. While I was at the Hospice, two of the monks, accompanied by four dogs, started off on their daily errand of mercy. It was affecting to see what a human-like interest and eagerness the dogs apparently took in their duty; and, as I watched them go out in the dismal, dreary cold of the Alpine snows and the approaching night, I asked myself, "Could I go so cheerfully and so readily out of my way to do good?" This was an instance where dogs were my teachers, and I was very glad to learn from them.

These earlier incidents of my life have been recalled by a circumstance which took place a few days ago. A little girl of my acquaintance went with her brother on a visit to Raymond, N. H. When she returned home, the first thing she told her mother was, how happy she had been in making the acquaintance of Slago, an old brave family-dog, which had been so very kind to her. The mother asked her what had made the old dog so kind? And the little girl simply answered, "Oh! it was because I was kind to him myself. I spoke gently to him, and patted him, and so he loved me very much."

And thus it ever is; if we are kind, either to a dog, or to one of our species, *kindness will come back in return.* If the monks of St. Bernard were rough and cruel to the noble animals which share their exile, they would soon run away into other and wilder regions of the Alps, and be of no use to any one.

If you shout in a scolding tone of voice before an echoing cliff, the echo will be sure to come back scolding also; but speak gently and kindly, and the echo will be gentle and kind.

THE MISSIONARY FAMILY.

I SHOULD like to take you with me in fancy, dear children, on a long voyage. Far away in the Southern Ocean, where the rays of the sun fall slantingly and feebly, and fragments of icebergs float like little white boats almost always on the dark waters, we should find the rocky coasts and rugged hills of the island I want you to visit, — the missionary island of Keppel. The little cottage of the missionary, the only house but one on the island, stands on a hill-side, and still lower down toward the shore are two small huts and a stable. A dreary and desolate place, you think, for which you would not like to leave your happy homes and gardens, your pleasant Sunday-schools, and your playmates.

The missionary family have none of these enjoyments. Their nearest neighbors live on the gray land you can just see, far to the south,—the Falkland Islands, where their father goes, once in a great while, to bring flour and provisions home. It is summer with them now, but you shiver at the chill wind, and wonder how they can bear it when their winter comes, with its cold, stormy winds, its short, dark days and long nights of frost. There are no trees on the island, only low shrubs and coarse grass, on which the cows are feeding, and thorny vines on which the large blackberries are ripening.

See! the house door is thrown open, and the missionaries' daughters have come out to gather the fruit. The two younger run on first, as full of life and enjoyment on their lonely island as any little girl at vacation; then follow the two elder ones with their fair, rosy, English faces, carrying the basket between them. But there is some other person coming up from one of the huts to go with them. She is a little dark-skinned woman, with black hair, which her husband has just braided neatly for her, and who seems rather uncomfortable in her new dress, for she is one of the natives from the Tierra del Fuego, to whom the missionary has been sent to teach them the glad tidings of a Saviour.

The younger girls are soon busy among the bushes with the native woman, whose name is too long and difficult for our lips to pronounce, and one of them stops now and then to drop a blackberry into the mouth of the little child of the native, who responds with "Cutta-cutta," meaning "Thank you," or, pulling at her dress, cries "Yamer, yamer," "Give me." The older girls are still on the hill, looking far over the sea toward the west, in the hope of seeing their father's ship, the "Allen Gardiner," with her white flag, bringing him home in safety from the Tierra del Fuego, where he has gone to bring back some more natives to be taught at the station. Well may they be anxious for him. But a few months ago, when he had been detained at home, the ship had been seized by the treacherous natives, and all but one man in her murdered. Still, the missionary perseveres in his work, thinking that the more wicked, cruel, and ungrateful the natives are, the more they need to hear of a holy God and a forgiving Saviour.

But the sun is setting, and the baskets are filled, and after gathering a handful of a delicate, sweet-scented, little white flower, to ornament their sitting-room, the girls run down to the wharf to meet their little brother. He has been fishing in a boat, with a native and an English lad who came out with them, and has an amusing account to give, of the brown hairy seals they have seen on a piece of ice, watching them with queer, intelligent faces. So they turn toward their home, where they share the duties and lighten the labors of their mother, for they can obtain no help there.

You would scarcely think, if you saw them working with active and skillful hands in the house, that not very many years ago I used to see them led by their nurses, through the wide hall of their English home, with its colored windows, into their father's drawing-room, that he might introduce the shy, fair little creatures, in their fresh white dresses, to his guests.

Do you wonder why their father brought them from that dear home, with its lovely garden and all its comforts, to live a life of labor on this lonely island? It was because he loved his God and Saviour, and when he heard that in the desolate land of Tierra del Fuego there were five thousand savages, who had never heard of God or heaven, who lived in ignorance and wickedness, killing and even eating each other, and dying without any knowledge of a life to come, he felt it his duty to leave his happy and comfortable home, and try to teach them of Jesus, and his love to sinners. And now, dear children, when you pray to the Saviour you have early learned to love, will you not remember to ask him to help and protect that missionary till some of these poor savages have learned to obey and love our Lord Jesus Christ?

NOT ALL FOR ONE.

A GERMAN FABLE.

A PEACOCK was strutting proudly round the domains of his owner, with his tail wide spread, when he espied a poor black raven on the dead limb of a tree. "Hoot, there! Be off, you shabby fellow!" he cried. "I'm the king over all winged gentlemen about here, and"—flapping his wings and mounting a huge stone gate-post—"this is my throne. I'll have no such mean gentry as you about."

"Caw, caw, caw!" cried the raven. "I think mine is a hard lot indeed; and I wonder what I was made for! Probably to afford fun for such grand birds as you! To be scorned and ordered from one tree to another! If I only had a voice like yonder nightingale, who is sleeping to make up for the time she lost in serenading last night, why, it would atone for my rusty coat and croaking voice! But, alas, I'm a poor, despised creature, and had better be out of the world than in it, unless I had a better fate!"

"Ah, sir," screeched the peacock, "you have one charm, which, as you do not seem to value or even to claim it, must belong to me,—those fine red boots on your legs! I've not the least doubt but they were made for me, to match my magnificent plumes; so off with them! Take these poor rusty ones I have on, and don't let me catch you thieving from gentlemen again, or I'll order you shot as a cherry-thief or a hen-robber!"

"Alas, alas, what a fate is mine!" croaked again the raven. "Will he tear the red boots, my only charm, from off my legs?" "Indeed I will, and the voice from out the throat of that lady in the nest, too! I am very sure that he who gave me these splendid plumes never intended that I should go about without a voice and a pair of boots to correspond with them! You and the nightingale are *nobody* now; and you could not be less if you yield me my rights." And with this fine speech the gentleman turned himself round and round, that the sun might glisten among his feathers while he waited for *his* boots, as he called them.

"Caw, caw, caw!" croaked the raven. "What is to become of me? I'll be stripped of my one only charm if I stay, and

I'll be shot for a thief if I attempt to fly! I wish I'd never been hatched!"

Now, during all this conversation, a poor dull toad had been in the garden-beds near by, picking up his breakfast of bugs and worms. He was amazed at the scornful pride of the peacock, as well as at the miserable discontent of the raven. He knew that he was one of the humblest creatures the Lord of the garden ever made; but he resolved to rebuke his superiors for this spirit of rebellion. "Look at me, friends," he whispered, in a voice scarcely audible; "what have I to boast of? I am the meanest creature that ever came from the great Father's hand, so men say. I have no gay plumes nor red boots to delight the eye, no voice to charm the ear. My eyes are dull and swollen, my whole form is loathsome; so that delicate ladies and little children run from my presence and shriek if I hop—for I can not even walk—toward them. And yet the good Lord has not overlooked even *me;* to me he has given *life*, with the power of enjoying his air and his sunshine. For this I will bless him, rather than call in question his wisdom in forming me the unlovely thing that I am. I know not for what I am placed here, nor yet do the men who spurn me know; but it is very certain that the All-wise has made nothing in vain. Doubtless I have a corner to fill, a work to do which would suit no other. Therefore will I thank my Maker for the sweet boon of life, and bow quietly to his will. Learn of me each to be content with his own mercies,—the peacock with his plumes, the raven with his boots, and I who have nothing else, with *life*;—remembering that he who doeth all things well gives not unto any one of his creatures all his good things; but divides them according to his wisdom." And with one leap the poor, humble teacher escaped from their sight and hid himself under the broad leaves of the waving corn.

CHARLIE RAY'S TROUBLES.

"It is so very, very hard to be good," said Charlie Ray, mournfully, holding his hot cheeks in his little fat, dimpled hands.

"Yes; it is very hard indeed," said his mother, in a sympathizing tone; "I think I should get discouraged myself if God had not promised to help me when I ask him."

"But God is *so far off*," said Charlie, though in a tone less sad; and now he rested those feverish cheeks in his mother's hands.

"Yes, so far off that he is present in the most distant star of night, but so near, so very near, Charlie, that he is by your side to know your most secret thoughts."

"But it can not be so hard for grown-up people to do right, —why can not I wait till I am older?"

"Why, Charlie!" interrupted Mrs. Ray; "you forgot to change your shoes."

Charlie hung his head. "Why, you see, mother, I have got so much into the habit of not changing them that I forgot, though I do try to remember."

"From this, then, you see why it is very important for you to get into the habit of doing right when you are a little boy, or it will be very hard for you to begin to do right when you are a man."

"I never thought of that," said Charlie, eagerly; "so it may be harder for a man to do right than for me!"

"Yes, but remember if you get into the habit of doing right now, it will be easier for you to do right when you are a man."

"So it will," exclaimed Charlie, with delight, "and I will try."

"But, besides this, you must not think you will have less temptations when you are older. You do little things to help me now, because you are a little boy; when you are larger and do more, your work will not seem harder to you than it does now, for you will have more strength to do it. So, now, it seems to you that you have great temptations and little strength to meet them; when you are older, you will have greater temptations and greater strength to meet them."

"But, mother," and Charlie hesitated, "it does not seem as if God knew just how very hard it is for such a little boy to do just right."

"Who is Jesus Christ?"

"God the Son."

"And Jesus Christ was once a little boy in Nazareth, and knew all a little boy's troubles. He knew what it was to have his playmates sometimes ill-natured and selfish, and therefore just how hard you find it always to be kind and generous. Think, then, when you are troubled and tempted, that we are told,—'He was tempted in all points like as we are,' that he might help us when tempted; and that he knows just how hard a little boy like you finds it to do right. Ask for help for the sake of the holy child Jesus."

"And I too can think," said Charlie's brother Henry, "that he was once a young man in Galilee. You, dear mother, good and kind as you are, can not know all a young man's trials and temptations, but Jesus Christ does. Thank you for this thought. Oh, how it will strengthen me to think of Jesus Christ not only as the Wonderful, the Counselor, the Son of God, but as the young man who was pure and holy, not only in his country life among the hills of Galilee, but amid the stronger enticements of the great city. Thank God not only that he died for men, but that he lived among them. Thank God for his boyhood and youth, as well as busy manhood."

WORKING FOR IMMORTALITY.

One of the old masters in sculpture was noted for the length of time he always spent upon his works. So fine was his eye for the beautiful, that it seemed he would never be satisfied till the form before him should move and breathe.

At one time he was longer than usual over a cetain subject in which he was all absorbed. The gray dawn found him before the marble, and the shadows of twilight fell upon him still there, with chisel in hand. Again and again it was pronounced finished; but still he saw a touch wanting here and a line there, and went to work with all the devotion of the artist to a fresh subject. Thus did he renew his toil through many a day, and far into the small hours of night. A friend, to whose less practiced eye the work seemed already perfect, ventured to expostulate with him on what appeared to be a waste of time. "Why," he asked, "do you spend so much time and labor upon that one statue?" "Because," replied the sculptor, "I am working *for immortality*."

All we, in a higher sense than this, are working for immortality. We are forming characters for eternity. Every word, every thought, every action, makes a line or a touch far more enduring than that of the chisel upon the sculptor's marble. Nor is it upon our own hearts only that the influence of our work is seen. If some touch of ours has left a line of beauty upon another, it shall live there for ever; if we have marred the form we should have graced, the blemish shall also live and reflect its unseemliness upon us again. Whether we would have it thus or not, so it is; all our work is for immortality. The material upon which *character* is wrought is more abiding than granite. It will survive when earth itself, and all it contains, shall have passed away. Oh, how important that we take for our model Jesus,—the holy, the pure, the beautiful; and that we touch and retouch our work until we see in ourselves his blessed likeness! Let us also aim to reproduce his features on all around; then shall our labors shine forth glorious in their immortality. Well will it be for us, when we meet the products of life and labor in eternity, if there be none upon whom, by our example or direct influence, we have wrought a dark line or an unsightly shade. If God has kept us so that no dear buried heart bears the impress of our neglect or unkindness, let us pray that all our work in the future may be done in love; so that we may rejoice to know that it is done for immortality.

ANNIE'S DISOBEDIENCE.

One pleasant Saturday afternoon, Annie Stone received her mother's permission to visit a young friend, and stay to tea. She was not often permitted this indulgence, and now she was highly delighted. Her anticipations of happiness were so great, that it was rather difficult to wait patiently for her playmate Mary Ann, who was to accompany her. At last she came, and as they were going, Mrs. Stone said, "Annie, you know that Angeline lives very near the river. Remember that you must not go to the water, or get into a boat, because, if you should, you might get hurt, or perhaps drowned." Annie promised to obey, and with light hearts and nimble feet the little girls were soon out of sight.

Their half-mile walk led them through the pleasant village, along the bank of the river, and their attention was constantly occupied with something new and interesting. When they arrived at their young friend's house, they found two other little girls, who made a pleasant addition to the party, and all played happily together.

After an early tea, Harriet Bailey, one of the girls, said, "Come, let us go down to the vessel. My father is going to sea in it, and I visit it every day." But Annie said, "Oh, no. My mother told me not to go to the water because I might get drowned."

"No, you won't," replied Harriet. "I know just where to go." Annie hesitated, but finally, rather than remain alone, she allowed herself to be persuaded, and followed on after them.

The vessel did not lie close by the wharf, and, for the convenience of those who had business on board, a plank had been laid across. When Annie looked down into the deep, dark water she was afraid, and shrunk back; the others had no fears, and they took hold of her hand and led her safely over. The men who were about the vessel had finished their work for the day and gone home. There being none to restrain them, the young visitors ran about, looking at every thing, and peeping into every strange place. Annie did not feel quite as happy as the others. She could not forget her mother's command, and knew that she was doing wrong.

Dear children, think of the kind parents God has given you. They love you, and require only what will make you happy. It may not always seem so to you, but they know better than you do. Avoid the first wish to do wrong; this is sin, and will lead you on step by step to ruin. Imitate Jesus. He was always obedient to his father and mother, though he was Immanuel. Do this, and it will make you happy.

Night was fast approaching, yet the little girls were so much occupied that they did not notice it. "There was a great hole here in my father's vessel," said Annie, "where they put down barrels." "Oh, no," said they, "there is none here;" but Annie was right; the hatchway was now open, and many loads of stones had that day been thrown into the hold for ballast. In the darkness, the children did not see it, and suddenly Annie plunged headlong down — down — struck on the stones, and became insensible. When consciousness returned, she heard Mary Ann calling her, and found that she, too, had fallen. "Are we in the river?" said Annie, for her face and hands were wet. "No," replied her companion, "we are down in the bottom of the vessel." Annie cried, and said they never should get out. How sadly she felt when she remembered that disobedience to her mother had brought this suffering upon her. Mary Ann was not much hurt, and by getting up on the pile of stones she could see a little light from above. After what seemed a very long time to the poor children, they heard a strange voice calling, "Children, where are you?" and a man with a lantern in his hand looked down from the deck. It was Harriet's father, who, having heard of the accident, had come to the vessel, and was greatly relieved to find the little girls alive.

After Annie was rescued, she was found to be covered with blood which flowed from a deep cut on her head, and soon became insensible again. Assistance was obtained, and she was immediately carried home. It would be difficult to describe the alarm of Mrs. Stone when the door opened, and two men entered bringing Annie in their arms, pale and covered with blood. The physician came, carefully examined the wound, and dressed it. Though she was suffering much pain, Annie bore it patiently; she felt that she deserved it, and that God had punished her for disobeying her kind mother.

Dear children, is not this story of disobedience a sad one? Annie never forgot the lesson. She is now herself a mother, and often, when wishing to impress the duty of obedience upon her children, she relates this event in her history, and shows the long white scar on her head, which time can never efface. Little friends, when you wish to do what your parents have forbidden, remember that disobedience will sooner or later be punished. Look to Jesus for help to do what is right. Say,—

"Heavenly Shepherd, please to watch us,
Guard us both by night and day;
Pity show to little children,
Who like lambs too often stray.

"We are always prone to wander;
Please to keep us from each snare;
Teach our infant hearts to praise thee
For thy kindness and thy care."

THE LITTLE SOLDIER.

"Oh, would I were a soldier,"
Cried little Bertie Lee;
"If I were only older,
How very brave I'd be;
I'd fear not any danger,
I'd flee not from the foe,
But where the strife was fiercest,
There I'd be sure to go.

"I'd be the boldest picket,
 Nor fear the darkest night;
Could I but see a rebel,
 How bravely I would fight;
I'd nobly do my duty,
 And soon promoted be—
Oh, would I were a soldier,"
 Sighed little Bertie Lee.

"But when I'm grown to manhood,
 This war will all be o'er,
I can not join this struggle,
 Our dear flag to restore,
I may not bleed for freedom,
 That glory's not for me;
My name will not be written,
 The hero, Herbert Lee."

Then answered Bertie's mother,
 In tender, loving tone,
"My darling little Bertie,
 You need not thus bemoan.
A nobler strife awaits you,
 'Tis even now begun,
And you may gain the victory,
 If brave and true, my son.

"You *are* a little soldier,—
A picket guard, my boy,
To ward off every evil
That may your soul annoy.
No earthly foe need vex you,
No midnight sounds alarm,—
With Jesus for your leader,
What could my darling harm?

"The noblest of all soldiers
My little son may be,
His name *in heaven* recorded,
The hero, Herbert Lee.
That were far higher glory
Than any earthly fame;
God grant the list '*Promoted*'
May bear my Bertie's name."

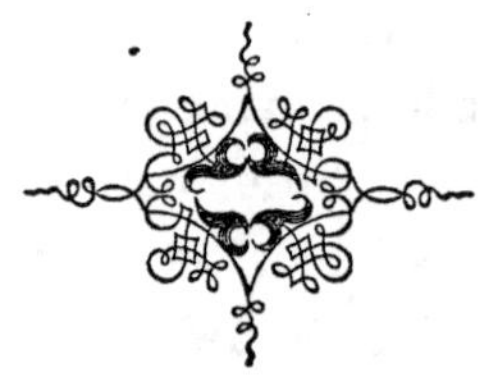

"THE ONLY NEW THING I'VE GOT."

LITTLE Henry, a boy of five years old, loved to sit beside his mother and watch the progress of a pretty pair of scarlet mittens. To his oft-repeated inquiry, "Whom are they for?" she replied, "A good little boy." After they were finished, she laid them away, satisfying his eager solicitations by telling him, if Henry proves "a good little boy," he will find them hanging upon the family Christmas-tree with his name interwoven in the wrist.

In the mean time, a contribution for a Home Missionary's family was being made. Henry's mother, upon her return from the ladies' meeting, informed her little son what they were engaged in. After giving him some information respecting the missionary's children, she said, "Well, Henry, what will *you* give for some one of these children?" After thinking a few moments, he replied, "I'll send my *new mittens* to that little boy of the missionary so near my age." His mother said, "And go without all winter? Perhaps mamma will not get time to knit any more, although she would be so glad to do so." His little chin quivered, and his eyes filled with tears.

He hesitated a moment, and then said, "Yes, if mamma will sew up my old ones." Upon being assured that his old ones should be mended, his countenance lighted up again. Upon the entrance of his sister, he made known to her his intention.

"What! send your *new mittens!* and not have any on the Christmas-tree!" His head dropped again; he made no reply. But his mother answered; "Let him do just as he has a mind to." Soon after, his father and a favorite sister entered. His mother said in a cheerful tone, "Papa, Henry has concluded to send his new mittens to the missionary's little boy." His sister, surprised, unconsciously said, "Why, no, Henry; I would not send my little mittens; I would send something else!" He stood a moment, with downcast look, evidently in a deep struggle of mind, when suddenly he looked up to his mother, and, with a sorrowful and tremulous tone, said, "Then I can't send any thing, for my little mittens are the only *new thing* I've got!"

WHO TAUGHT THEM?

The Bible never attempts to prove the existence of God. It takes that for granted. In the very first verse, instead of formally declaring "There is a God," it says, "*God* created the heaven and the earth."

But, dear children, there are some, even in this land of

Bibles, this land in which God has so wonderfully shown his handiwork, breathing a benediction of beauty on every tree and shrub and flower that rejoices in the glad sunlight, who say they do not believe there is any God, and many more who act as if they did not believe it.

Let me tell you of one such person, in the words (as nearly as I can) of the Sabbath-school superintendent from whom I first heard the story.

"A short time since, a gentleman, conversing of his recent visit to South America, spoke of an interview with a young man, whom he had formerly known in New York.

This young man, like many others, having had more money than good counsel left him by his parents, soon became very self-sufficient. To show his independence, he began by breaking the Sabbath; and as one step in the downward road always leads to the second, he went on from one vice to another till he reached open infidelity, and remained thus when he left New York for South America.

But when this gentleman met him, the avowed infidel had become the humble believer in Jesus Christ, and the tongue that was wont to blaspheme was lifting the voice of supplication for the blessing of God upon his guilty soul.

Greatly surprised at seeing the young man "clothed and in his right mind," the gentleman inquired what had wrought the change.

Said he, "You know I spent much of my time in fishing and hunting, and a few weeks since, on a beautiful Sabbath morning, I went in search of game. Being weary of roaming about the woods, I sat down on a log to rest. While thus seated, my attention was attracted to a neighboring tree, by the cries of a bird which was fluttering over her nest, uttering shrieks of anguish as if a viper were destroying her young.

"On looking about, I soon found the object of her dread, a venomous snake, crawling slowly toward the tree, his eye intent on the bird and her nest. Presently I saw the male bird coming from a distance with a little twig covered with leaves in his mouth. Instantly the mother-bird dropped upon her nest, and the male bird laid the twig over his mate and her young, and then perched himself on one of the topmost branches of the tree, awaiting the arrival of the enemy.

"By this time the snake had reached the spot. Coiling himself around the trunk, he ascended the tree and at length, gliding along the branch till he came near the nest, he lifted his head as if to take his victims by surprise. He looked at the nest, then suddenly drew back his head as if he had been shot, and hurriedly made his way down the tree as best he might.

"I had the curiosity to see what had turned him from his malicious purpose; and on ascending the tree, I found the twig to have been broken from a poisonous bush which that snake was never known to approach.

"Instantly the thought rushed across my mind, 'Who taught that bird its only weapon of defense in this hour of peril?' and quick as the thought came the answer 'None but God Almighty, whose very existence I have denied, but in whose pardoning mercy, through Jesus Christ, I am now permitted to hope.'"

"Are not two sparrows sold for a farthing? and one of them shall not fall to the ground without your Father. Fear not, therefore, ye are of more value than many sparrows."

Oh, then, dear children, when the Evil One comes to that hallowed spot, your own quiet home, to devour your souls by scattering the seeds of discord and strife among your happy circle, pray to him who heareth the young ravens when they cry, that some kind messenger from yonder spirit land may be commissioned to bring you protection from the destroyer, that so you may "dwell in the secret place of the Most High, and abide under the shadow of the Almighty."

THE GOOD FIGHT OF FAITH.

"Mamma, how do they fight the good fight of faith?" asked Nellie.

"Can either of these boys answer Nellie's question?" asked her mother, addressing Allen and Freddy, who were present. Allen who was in raptures over a new bow and arrow which his grandfather had given him, thought that was the weapon used. Freddy was quite sure it was fought with swords like Captain B.'s, which flashed and glittered in the sun, and he thought he should like to fight the good fight of faith if his father would buy him such a sword.

Nellie had remained quite silent during the expression of these opinions, apparently deep in thought. Suddenly a bright idea entered her mind, and she exclaimed, "I know now, mamma; they fight the good fight of faith with pistols, because you know we read of Paul's pistols." Mamma explained to Nellie that what she had thought pistols were epistles, or letters written to the several churches, though she was quite willing to admit that these same epistles had fired many a shot which had wounded the King's enemies, and brought them on their knees to acknowledge his rightful authority. "You have not yet told me against what enemies these weapons are used," said Mrs. D——, anxious to draw out the opinions of her children, that she might adapt her instructions accordingly.

"I think," said Freddy, "that it is the Secessionists."

Nellie could not think who they could be; apparently she had exhausted her mental powers when she conceived the brilliant idea of the pistols. Mrs. D—— explained that most of the battles in the good fight of faith were fought not with Secessionists, but with the sins in our own hearts, and that the weapon used was God's truth, the sword of the Spirit. She proposed to the children that they should begin immediately to fight against these sins; and, lest they should be discouraged, she recommended that they take only one at a time.

"What shall I commence with?" said Nellie.

"I think," said Mrs. D——, "that you should commence with indolence." Nellie hung her head in shame, for she was now eight years old, and could not read without spelling half her words, because she had been too idle to study.

"How shall I begin?" said Freddy.

"You must watch against untruthfulness," said Mrs. D——. "I have observed that you will sometimes screen yourself from blame by telling what is not true."

"Mamma, I do not think I have any sins to fight against," said Allen, "for I do not tell wrong stories and I am not indolent." Mamma was not long in convincing Allen that this extremely good opinion of himself was entirely erroneous; and she pointed out to him that fretfulness was his besetting sin, and one that was extremely annoying to others. Perhaps I will tell you at some future day how these little soldiers succeeded in fighting the good fight of faith.

GRETA AND THE FLOWERS.

Little Greta, pale and weary,
  Fainteth in the city air;
Longing for the breezy country—
  Her fond mother bears her there.

Never had the eyes of Greta
  Watched a bud from day to day,
With its perfumed leaves unfolding,
  In God's own mysterious way.

So, although the snow-white ox-eye
  Long had *budded* 'mid the grain,
Seeking late and seeking early,
  Greta sought a *flower* in vain;

Till the little maiden, waking
  Once in light of early day,
Gazing on the pleasant meadow,
  And the pastures far away,

Sees the rows of snowy ox-eyes
  Waving in the morning air;—
(Never had the child in visions
  Dreamed or thought of aught so fair;—)

Cries she now with joyous laughter,
"Mother, rise and look about;
Early have the busy fairies
Hung their tiny washing out."

THE LITTLE FACE IN NORTON ALLEY.

"Come, my dear, put your book away and take a walk with me," said Mrs. Cooper to her little daughter one October day, when October was beautifully glorious with color and sunshine.

"Where are you going, mamma?"

"To Norton Alley."

"It's a mean place, mother."

"No, it is only a poor place, and I wish you to go."

"What for?"

"I am going in search of little boys or girls for the Sunday school."

"Oh, I don't wish to go; I am reading the nicest little book that ever was written."

"Well, your book will wait until you come back. I wish to show you an unwritten book."

"What is an unwritten book?"

"Come, and I will show you."

"There! I told you it was mean," said Alice, as soon as they came within the alley; "just look at those children,—they are ragged and dirty, and look as if they liked it."

"So would you be if you had had no one to teach you that it is better to be tidy and clean."

"I can't believe it, mother."

"It is only true; if you had always lived in this alley and played with children like these, vou would not know the difference."

Mrs. Cooper called one of the little girls to her. "What is your name?" she asked.

"Gertrude, that's my name."

"Have you ever been in Sunday school, Gertrude?"

"I don't know where 'tis, ma'am; is it like the circus where they jumps on the horses that runs?" asked the child.

Alice laughed, and Gertrude grew very red and angry, as she said, "*You* needn't to laugh at me; the circus is the only place I knows anything about."

"My little girl shall not laugh at you," said Mrs. Cooper, "and I will tell you what kind of a place the Sunday school is. It is a nice large room, with pictures on the walls, and seats in it, where many little boys and girls go every Sunday, and are taught how to read a book that tells them what they must do in this world if they would go to heaven when they die."

"Die! die!" repeated the child; "why, that's what Bobby's been doing."

"Where is he?"

"Come, and I'll show you; he looks as if he'd been whitewashed, and he won't get up a bit; mother's been calling him all day, and I don't believe a bit as he can hear what she says; come right on, and I'll show him to you."

"No! no! Gertrude," called Mrs. Cooper, "you may tell your mother that there is a lady here who would like to come in."

"Don't go, don't, mother," pleaded Alice; "it's so dirty and mean."

"This is only one leaf of the book," said her mother; "come and look at it."

Alice drew back, and looked as if she would run away if she had the courage. Gertrude came from a house near by, a moment later, and said, "You may come if you're a mind to, 'cause she don't take no notice of me, no more nor if I wasn't there."

Gertrude led the way into the house, followed by Mrs. Cooper and Alice.

Over a little form bent the mother, who was sobbing piteously, and neither moved nor spoke when Mrs. Cooper went in.

"When did the little boy die?" asked a sweet voice of the bending mother. It aroused her. She lifted herself up and turned her tearful eyes upon Mrs. Cooper, only murmuring, "He's dead, — he's gone, like all the rest; my last one, — my little boy."

"When did he go?"

"He died in the night."

"Shall I wash the little face for you?" asked Mrs. Cooper.

"Thank you, ma'am; I suppose it ought to be done."

"Don't, mother, don't touch it!" whispered Alice; "I shall be afraid to kiss you to-night if you do."

"Very well, my dear, you may not kiss me, but you may go home as quickly as you can, and tell nurse that there is a little boy dead here, and I wish her to come to me with whatever she thinks I may need."

Alice did not wait for a second bidding. She ran out of the alley as swiftly as she could.

"Look here, what's your name?" called Gertrude, who had followed Alice.

"My name is Alice. Where are you going?"

"With you, to see whereabouts you live."

"You had better not," said Alice; and poor Gertrude turned back with a sad face.

Alice hastened home and reported the case to nurse, who made the needful preparations, and, with her hat on, stopped to ask, "Are you not going with me? I do not know the way."

Alice had thought the disagreeable duty done, and had opened the "nicest story-book in the world." She closed it, and went with nurse.

Gertrude was sitting on the floor beside the bed, looking intently at the face of her little brother.

"Why, mamma, how pretty he is!" exclaimed Alice, as she saw the change her mother had wrought in the face of the dead child; "he looks more as if the angels would take him into heaven now," she said.

"Don't they let no folks go into that place if they haven't clean faces?" asked Gertrude,—"'cause I'll go out to the pump and wash mine quick, if that'll let me in."

"It is clean hearts that we must have to go there," said Mrs. Cooper, as she lifted the dead darling gently from his mother's arms, and prepared to robe him in his last little dress.

"It's pretty!" said the mother, and she put her hand on the dress nurse had brought, and for an instant looked up into Mrs. Cooper's face.

"Yes, it was my Willie's dress," she said.

"Haven't you him now?"

"No," said Mrs. Cooper, and a tear-drop found its way to Willie's little dress.

"Why—where?" and the newly-bereaved mother could ask no more.

"I am glad, I am thankful," said Mrs. Cooper, "Willie has

gone to heaven; we ought always to be happy when they are there, you know."

"Do you think they'd let my Bobby in?"

"I know he is safely there."

"How can you tell?" And the mother looked up eagerly; she had forgotten for an instant the present clay.

"Because Jesus has promised it."

"Jesus! Jesus! Is he like God?"

"He is God's own dear Son," said Mrs. Cooper; "and the soul of little Bobby is safe with him in heaven."

"I wish I'd known, I wish I'd known, so's I could tell him when he looked so frightened," said the poor woman. "Look, ma'am, Bobby was little, Bobby never did naughty things; how shall *I* ever get where he's gone?"

"Why, mother, don't you know?" said Gertrude; "the lady says we must have clean hearts, but I don't see how we can wash them, for they're all covered up tight."

"*We* can't wash them; it is Jesus who washes them with his blood, if we ask him," said Mrs. Cooper.

Gertrude sat still on the floor, looking very much puzzled at these new things, and Alice began to think that it was very beautiful of her mother to make Bobby look so nice.

"I will come again in the morning and see you," said Mrs. Cooper, as, having made the dead child ready for its burial, she kissed the cold face, and bade the mother good-by.

"Mayn't I kiss him too,—he looks like Willie?" asked Alice, turning back from the door. The child kissed the white forehead, and, touched by her mother's kindness, a little of it crept into her own heart. "You may come with me now, and I will show you where we live," she said to Gertrude, "if your mother will let you."

"We will wait until to-morrow, and then she may come," said Mrs. Cooper, "for now I am not going home."

"Where?" asked Alice, when they were again in the alley.

"You shall see," said her mother; and Alice saw a little coffin bought for Bobby; and the following day she tied a wreath of flowers that lay over Bobby's still little heart, and then they took him out of Norton Alley, and laid him in the pure, fresh earth, until the time when God shall send out his angels to gather in his lambs.

PATSY.

THE children had been playing one summer afternoon in the grassy lane that led down to the little cottage where Uncle Tim lived. There were Fanny and Mabel and Bessy White and Eunice, the youngest, whom they called "little Tuney," and Patsy, a little colored girl, whose mother used to wash and iron for Mrs. White. Merry as the butterflies which they chased, were these children, — all but Patsy. Not that she was not as active as any of the others, but she was not allowed to join in their plays; and when she attempted to do so, she was repelled in an unkind manner, which brought the tears into her eyes, and the big painful sobs into her bosom.

Uncle Tim had been sitting in the shade near the door of his house enjoying the soft warm air of the afternoon, and watching the play of the children. He was old and lame, but he had a kind heart. Long years before, he had had a little pet, — his Minnie, — but the bud did not remain to blossom, for God took it to plant in his own garden above. Perhaps he had been thinking of her this afternoon, for his eye was moist, and his look was very gentle, so that when the merry players ran that way, he called them to him, and spoke so pleasantly that they came at once where he was sitting.

"What is the matter," he asked, "with Patsy?" "Oh!" said Mabel, "she cried because Bessy White called her names and pushed her away."

"Ah," said he, "I am sorry to hear that! Why did you do so, Bessy?"

"Because she is black, and we don't want *such* with us."

"Indeed!" replied Uncle Tim, at the same time calling the

timid little Patsy to his knee, "is that all? I am sorry that you are learning this lesson of unkindness so early. This is not obeying what the Saviour says, 'Do unto others as you would have them do to you.'"

Bessy said nothing, but hung down her head, and Uncle Tim proceeded:—

"Suppose that God had made you like Patsy, and somebody despised you for it, and called you names, and treated you unkindly, would you not feel very much hurt by it?"

"You say that Patsy is black;—but she can't help that; and it is only the color of the skin after all. Don't you think she has a soul within just as you have? Can she not learn to read and spell and sing, and do all such things as well as you?"

"Oh!" cried little Tuney, pushing her chubby face forward from behind Bessy, "Patsy spelled a big word in the school yesterday, and Miss Jones praised her for it, and gave her a little book."

"Well, that was right," said he, and, dropping his voice to a gentler tone, he continued, "Didn't Christ die for her just as he did for you; and if she loves him, won't he take her to his beautiful home in heaven and give her a shining crown and a snow-white robe and let her live with him for ever? And now will you be unkind to Patsy, and despise her because God made her what she is?"

Poor Bessy! — she felt the reproof. Bessy had a kind heart and didn't *mean* to do wrong, but she had seen similar conduct in people older than she was, and had learned too early the bad example. But she now resolved that she would be more careful not to hurt Patsy's feelings again; and after this, when any of her playmates did so, she interposed with Uncle Tim's question, "Didn't Christ die for her, and doesn't he love her just the same?"

LITTLE MATTY; OR, WHAT IS IT TO BE WORTH HALF A MILLION?

MATTY was a little boy, three or four years of age, whose noble and large-hearted father had died leaving him worth a great deal of money; but he left him something far better than that. Some of my little readers will wonder what could be better than a great many thousand dollars, with which a little boy could buy all the marbles, tops, base-balls, or foot-balls, all the kites, tops, or candies that he might choose.

But little Matty had one thing better than all his money, and that was a wise and good mother. She taught him about a Father in heaven, who was far better, even, than the father whose body they had laid away in the ground.

She taught him that if he loved this good and kind Father, and obeyed him, he would sometime go and live with him for ever. She also taught him much more than this; but she never told him that he was worth any more money than the poorest boy that came to their door for bread.

At the time of which we speak, Matty began to go to school, and to play with boys who had heard of his great wealth, and who felt that it was a very fine thing to be worth so much money. One afternoon, as Matty returned from school, a great change was seen in his manner, and he ordered the servants about as he had never done before.

None of them could tell what had happened, that a little boy, who had always before been so lovely and amiable, should so suddenly put on such important airs.

The secret, however, was soon revealed, for, as Matty met with some reproof from his faithful old nurse, with all his newly acquired dignity he said, "I am worth half a million."

Astonished at such words from Matty, she hastened to his pious mother with the news of the change which had come over her only son. Matty was immediately summoned, and, although much of his self-importance vanished as he entered the presence of his best earthly friend, yet he still showed that some unhappy influence was at work upon his little heart.

"Matty, my son, what is this that I hear of you?" said his dear mother.

"I am worth half a million," replied Matty.

With a sad and even grieved expression the mother continued, "What do you say, Matty?"

Matty's look was more subdued as he replied, "*The boys say* I am worth half a million."

"Well, Matty, what is it to be worth half a million?"

This was something that Matty did not so well understand, and his handsome and animated face became suddenly very thoughtful. He knew that it was something very important, for the words and manner of his play-fellows had plainly shown this to be the case, but what it was to be "worth half a million" he could not tell.

After a few moments' silent thoughtfulness, Matty, looking up into his mother's face, with a sweet and loving expression, replied, "Dear mamma, I don't know, unless it is to be a good boy, and go to Sabbath school."

GANPATI; AN IDOL GOD.

THE children will be pleased to know that this picture is a copy of one which was sent to us for them from Bombay, in India. It was accompanied by the following letter, which tells about the picture, and also gives some interesting facts about India.

My dear Children: India is a land full of idols. Some of them are very large, and made of stone; others are small, and made of brass, or silver, or gold, and others still are printed on paper. This morning I sent a little boy out to buy the picture of a god, so that you might see what strange things these poor ignorant people worship. Just look at that picture! A man's body with four arms and an elephant's head. The Hindoos call it Ganpati.

But do the people really worship such images in India? Certainly they do, every day. Although the images never move and never speak, yet the people are afraid of them. Generally, they think the image itself is a god, though some think there is a god in the image. Parents teach their children to believe this, and so all become idolaters.

Not long ago, a native Christian went into the house of a man who was making images like this picture, and when he came home, he told me the following story. The idol-maker had a little boy five or six years old, who sat watching his father and hearing the conversation. While they were talking, another man came in, and seeing one idol that was finished, he began to worship it. The little boy laughed, and running to him said,—

"What are you doing?—that is no god; father made it."

The father said,—"Hush, child, yes it is a god."

"But," the boy replied, "you just now took the clay and made it. How can it be a god?"

Then the father repeated two lines of poetry, very common among the Hindoos:—

"If you worship it, it's a god:
If you don't worship it, it's a stone."

The poor boy could not understand this, and he did not believe it, yet without stopping to say more, he ran merrily away repeating to himself what the father had just said.

Poor boy! He too will probably be an idol-maker, and like his father learn to worship the work of his own hands. Can we not do something for these poor children? Don't you think there would be room enough for them in heaven, if they should learn to love Jesus? I am sure there would, and I think all the angels would rejoice if they should see any of these children coming to heaven.

ELSIE'S BOOKS.

"Why, Elsie, what are you doing?" asked Miss Agnes, her governess, coming into the nursery one day after school. "Tearing the leaves out of your books? Why, you mustn't do so!"

Why not?" answered the little girl, pettishly, "they are my own to do what I please with; and I've read this one, and read it till I'm sick of it; so now I'm going to cut out all the pictures to paste in my scrap-book. I like that best of any thing."

"Yes, but my dear, it is wrong willfully to destroy any thing that may be of use to another. Only think how many poor little children there are in the world, who never had a story-book in their lives, who would be made happy for weeks, by the gift of one of those which you are destroying just for a fancy!"

"Children that never had a story-book!" repeated the little girl incredulously; "why, I never heard of such a thing! All the little girls I know have plenty; they wouldn't take these old things of mine if I offered them. I suppose you mean little beggars,—but they don't care about reading, do they?"

"Why, haven't they minds and hearts and souls, as well as other children? They would enjoy the treat of a pleasant story all the more because they have so few pleasures. I think if you would sometimes give one of the books you are tired of to the poor little beggars who come for cold victuals, it would make them very happy indeed, and perhaps help them to be good; for all your books teach how children should try to do right."

"I never thought about it before," said Elsie, looking down.

"And not only little beggars," said Miss Agnes; "but still more the poor children in alms-houses and hospitals and nurseries. Only think, Elsie, how many hundreds of children there are in such places in this great city; poor little orphans, most of them, whom kind people take care of, providing food and clothes, and a roof to shelter them, but not much else. You know it takes so much money to buy necessary things for so many little friendless creatures, that very little is left to buy books or playthings for them. And yet those children would enjoy such things just as much as others. How happy it would make some of them to have that very pile of nice story-books that you have gathered around you to cut up!"

"Well, Miss Agnes, and they shall!" exclaimed the warm-hearted child, her face glowing, and her eyes wet at this appeal to her sympathy. "If you'll only help me to get them to them! Poor little lonesome boys and girls with nothing to play with! We'll speak to mamma about it; but you know she lets me do just as I like with my things. I'm so glad you told me!"

Miss Agnes put her arm around the child, who had sprung to her side in her eagerness, and kissed her.

"Very well, my dear," she said; "then we will look over your shelves now; you have the most extensive library I ever saw, for a young lady of nine years! and we'll put together all you 'know by heart,' as you say, and ask your papa to let

John take the parcel to the Home for the Friendless to-morrow. That will be much better than cutting them up, won't it?"

"Oh, yes, Miss Agnes," said Elsie, blushing; "I'll never do such a selfish thing as that again! and I'll keep my papers too, —you know I always cut up my 'Child at Home,' and 'Reaper,' and all the rest for the pictures. But I will take care of every thing for the poor children now,—see if I don't! It will be so nice to give them a pleasure!"

"And it will give pleasure to some one else," said Miss Agnes, gravely. "Who was it, Elsie, who when he was on earth was one of the poor himself, who has given us special charge to be kind to the poor and needy, and share with them the good things his kindness has bestowed on us?"

"Jesus," said the little girl, reverently; "oh, Miss Agnes, I have been a very selfish girl,—I didn't think; but indeed, I never will waste my money and every thing so again; I will put it by for poor people; you will help me."

"Yes," said Miss Agnes, stroking her hair fondly; "and now we will set about our pleasant task."

GOING INTO A MINE.

This is a picture of coal miners, — men and boys, — going to their work. They are lowered, as you see, in a sort of box or basket, through that deep hole which leads to the mine, and which is called the shaft. When they reach the bottom, they will grope their way along, through those underground passages, with no light but what comes from the little lamps which they carry, until they reach the galleries where they work, and there they will stay, all through the day, returning to their homes above-ground at night.

It is a very dangerous calling. Sometimes the mines are suddenly overflowed with water, or there are explosions of gases, or the roof of the mine — that is the coal and earth above them — gives way, and, falling down, stops all the passages, so that the poor miners are buried alive. These accidents seldom, if ever, happen to the miners of our country, and not so often in England as formerly; but they do sometimes occur, and many lives are lost. So you see, these miners have need every day to commit themselves to the care of Him who can as easily see and watch over them, in their deep, dark working-places, as he can see us who are out in the light of the sun.

This picture is one of the illustrations of a book entitled, "Down in a Mine." It contains a most interesting story of a frightful accident which happened to five miners, three of whom were boys. The two men who were with them had the love of Christ in their hearts, and it is delightful to read how that love sustained these men in their dreadful trial, and enabled them to comfort their young companions. Truly, God is always ready to listen to the cry of those who put their trust in him. It also relates a second catastrophe in which all the workmen perished.

"SOW BESIDE ALL WATERS."

THE noonday train for Boston rushed into the station of one of our large inland towns, and, exhausted, stood panting for breath and lolling its hot, red tongue till water should be brought it. The passengers were lightly brushing the dust from their clothes, taking looks at each other, and wondering how long they must wait, when an unusual stir in the depot turned all eyes toward an advancing group. In a moment, several men stalked into the car, followed by one whose dress indicated his position as an army officer. Some of the new-comers quietly seated themselves, but the rest, packed three in a seat, entertained the company without by their loud jests and songs, some of which were more highly appreciated by the singers than by most of the passengers in the car.

The train having finished its lunch of wood and water, was ready to move on, which it did, amid the shouts of the by-standers, and the performance of the "Red, White, and Blue," by the noisy travelers.

"Who are these men?" was a question more easily asked than answered. Being accompanied by an officer, they must be on their way to do something in their country's service, but the apparent indifference of their farewells left little room for the thought that they were going into scenes of danger, to fight the battles of law and liberty. Yet they would make grand soldiers, so athletic and well-formed were they. Even the things which prevented their being a pleasant addition to a quiet car might make them of use in the field of battle. And sure enough, to the battles they were going, as was ascertained when the conductor appeared.

Still singing, each man, at one time, drew from his pocket a huge bit of uncooked, salt cod-fish, from which, after brandishing it as if it were a bowie-knife, he bit a piece. By this, one of their older and quieter companions seemed to be reminded that he, too, was not unprovided with "creature comforts," and out of his pocket came a little newspaper package, which, being opened, was seen to contain tobacco, evidently the parting gift of some boon companion.

Now all this, though not very agreeable, could have been very easily borne, especially as the men were just volunteering their services for their country's defense, had it not been for the profaneness of their conversation. The name which we are accustomed to take upon our lips only reverently in prayer, or lovingly in conversation, even that of the blessed Saviour, was lightly mentioned. This could not be endured. Many took refuge in the next car, but that was soon filled. The officer, who was a very young man, and had, as yet, no real authority over the volunteers, was probably afraid that if he reproved them, they would leave him at the next stopping-place; or he may have considered it as a matter of course that soldiers should swear. Whatever were his thoughts, he was silent on the subject.

The future defenders of the Constitution were in the midst of a song, rather a pretty one it was, about "the old red school-house," when a child left her place and went and stood by them as if listening. Her little head and heart, however, were full of something far more interesting to her than any song. She looked in each sunburnt, manly, though reckless, face, hesitated, retreated to her mother, who gave her an encouraging smile, returned to the men, stood a moment, then climbing on the seat at their backs, hastily thrust a pocket Testament into the hands of one of them, and scampered back to her mother

The little creature had been breathlessly watched in fearful hope, and now the unspoken prayers which, without doubt, had gone up from more than one heart for her success were changed to thanksgivings as the young man took the book, and after examining it with a pleased smile, put it carefully in his breast-pocket. His comrades wanted it. "No, it was given to me, and I will always keep it," said his face, and probably his tongue.

In a few minutes, the candy-boy passed, and the young man, with his little book still tightly buttoned under his coat, bought a paper of pop-corn, which he took across the car, and gave, with a kiss, to the little girl. Then he must have her to sit by him, not among his companions, but in another seat, where they talked together till the cars again stopped, and with a good-by kiss, the child left him and tripped lightly to the depot platform, where, with a sunny smile on her pretty face, she stood, waving another farewell.

A wonderful change had indeed passed over the men. Not one more oath had the child heard, and only two more profane words were uttered during the whole trip. Those men, with manly hearts beating under the rough exterior, could no more have been boisterous in her presence than could the doctors in the temple of old, in the presence of the wondrous boy who questioned them. After she passed out, there was a silence, broken at length by songs of a different nature from those sung at first; more patriotic and touching than comic. This was before the invention of the blasphemous "Hallelujah chorus." Had it been popular then, those men would not have sung it that afternoon. Though full of life and activity, and by their droll sayings amusing all about them, they grew less excited, and disposed to talk together of the parents and brothers left behind.

The little girl who so early began her missionary work — a work which no other person could have done — may never know, what others took pains to ascertain, to what regiment her Testament has gone, and when she hears of the different companies engaged on the field of battle, can only wonder if the little book, hidden in the breast-pocket, is laid beneath the green turf of Virginia; but God knows where it is. Without doubt, the seed which she cast on the deep, muddy waters of sin, as the Egyptians scattered their grain on the fields overflowed by the Nile, found a sure lodging-place, and by and by—it may not be till the great Harvest—when the angels will be the reapers, it shall come again to her.

LITTLE BY LITTLE.

One step and then another,
  And the longest walk is ended;
One stitch and then another,
  And the largest rent is mended;
One brick upon another,
  And the highest wall is made;
One flake upon another,
  And the deepest snow is laid.

So the little coral workers,
  By their slow but constant motion,
Have built those pretty islands
  In the distant dark blue ocean;
And the noblest undertakings
  Man's wisdom hath conceived
By oft-repeated efforts
  Have been patiently achieved.

THE HYBRID TREE.

THIS picture represents a strange and curious product of nature growing on the south side of the Taunton and Middleboro' Railroad, a few miles from Taunton. It is an apple-tree to the hight of six or eight feet, and an elm the rest of the way! None can explain how this strange thing was brought about. The phenomenon would be the more remarkable if either the apple portion or the elm portion or both were distinguished for quality or beauty. But in these respects there is certainly not much to recommend the singular partnership. The apples are not particularly fine, nor is the elm particularly vigorous or graceful, and the whole tree looks as if it knew it was a laughingstock to its fellows, and protested against the apparent attempt in its case to contradict the axiom in philosophy that two bodies can not be in the same place at the same time.

I have known men who reminded me of this hybrid tree. Well trained in boyhood, they began life with a disposition to do good for its own sake, and they did indeed bear fruit. For a while, their words and deeds were like "apples of gold in pictures of silver." But in the mean time there seems to have been another nature growing within them, and finally this came out in the form of a worldly ambition that proved too powerful for their simple Christian usefulness, and they shot up intrusively into public notice, sacrificing all but the relics of what they were, to affect a dignity which they could never quite reach. Better remain an apple-tree, though a very humble one, than undertake to be an apple-tree and an elm-tree in one, and finally make a failure of the whole tree.

THE GREAT CONQUEROR.

I SAW a mother, not long since, whose son had enlisted in the army. I expected to find her sad and disconsolate, for the young soldier was an only son, and was very much beloved at home. But to my surprise she was cheerful and happy.

"Merwin has gone," she said, "and I may never see him again; but I can not make myself unhappy about it. I have given him to God, and wherever the Lord's service takes him he must go. I know he will distinguish himself, wherever he is, for he has already proved himself a *great conqueror*."

"So young as he is!" I exclaimed; "how?"

"He has *conquered himself*," replied the mother; "and you know what the Bible says about that."

"Oh, yes indeed," said I; "but I thought your Merwin was one of those who find it very easy to be good. There is a great difference in children. Some are so amiable and gentle that when they become Christians you see but little change in their outward conduct, and some"—

"But my son was not one of those," said she, interrupting me. "He was born with a hot, fiery temper. It used to frighten me almost, when he was nothing but a baby, and I hardly dared to think what would become of him when he grew older. I prayed a great deal about it, and talked and labored to help him to overcome his naughty, passionate spirit. And he began very early to try to govern himself. I recollect when he was not more than four years old, he had been very much provoked about something, and I could see the fire kindling in his eye and the color rising in his cheek. But he kept very still until his anger had subsided, and then he came running to me, threw his arms around my neck, and, bursting into tears, he cried, 'Kiss me, mamma, kiss me; *I've overcome.*'"

"That's beautiful!" I exclaimed.

"Many a time," the mother continued, "have I seen him struggle with his hasty, angry feelings, until by degrees it grew easier for him to control his temper, and now I can truly say, I believe by the grace of God, he has conquered himself. And among the qualifications for good soldiership that is one of the very best, *I* think."

I thought so too, as I repeated to myself the words of the Bible, to which Merwin B.'s mother had alluded. You will find them, little reader, in Prov. xvi. 32: "He that is slow to anger is better than the mighty; and he that ruleth his spirit, than he that taketh a city."

And I felt as if I wanted all the little boys to become conquerors in this same sense. No matter if you are not called to be soldiers to march at the call of your country to the battle-field and fight. You may be called of God to conquer enemies elsewhere. You may be called to govern and direct others. Whatever may be your duty in life, the best preparation you can make is to learn to govern yourself.

An angry spirit is a terrible enemy. It comes upon you so suddenly that it takes you unawares, throws you off your guard, and has vanquished you before you have time to think. Then if you *are* on the watch, it is so strong, so furious, so unwilling to listen to the voice of reason, that if you are not well armed, and if you have not helpers close by, you are most likely to be beaten. So, dear boys, it becomes you to be on the lookout all the while for it. As Jesus said, "Watch and pray, lest ye enter into temptation." You must have your armor on too, always. Never venture to lay it aside for a moment. If you do, you will, I am sure, be overcome. And more than all, do not live very far away from God, who alone is able to make you conqueror over this dreadful enemy. If you live near to him, he will protect you. He will "teach your hands to war, and your fingers to fight;" will encourage you in the heat of the conflict with his smile and whispers of comfort and love, and will give you the victory. Better than all, he will bring you at last up to his own home, put a crown upon your head, and seat you upon a throne of glorious triumph in the heavenly kingdom of Jesus Christ; for hear what Jesus has said: "To him that overcometh will I grant to sit with me in my throne, even as I also overcame, and am set down with my Father in his throne."

THE PILGRIM MONUMENT.

Every child has heard of Plymouth Rock, and of the Pilgrims who landed there. It was on the 22d of December,

1620. The picture shows the very large and costly monument which is being built at Plymouth to commemorate that event.

The monument is to be one hundred and fifty feet high, built of solid granite. The figure at the top is a statue of Religion holding an open Bible, and pointing to heaven. The figures below, two of which only are seen, are Morality, Education, Law, and Liberty. Underneath these are representations of the "Departure from Delfthaven," "The signing of the Social Compact in the Cabin of the May-Flower," "The Landing at Plymouth," and "The First Treaty with the Indians." On the four large panels are the names of the Pilgrims and the principal events in their history.

It is a good thing to erect monuments of good men. Our Pilgrim Fathers were such men. They loved religion, and they came here to have a home where they could worship God without molestation. And as they honored God, so he has honored them. He has made of that little company a great nation, who recall with pride and veneration their memory. Let us, as we enjoy our dear homes and our blessings, thank God for the Pilgrims, and that we are now reaping the fruits which they sowed for us in prayer and faith and suffering, almost two hundred and fifty years ago.

THE TRUANT SKATER.

When the trees with ice were laden,
  And the north wind loudly blew,
Edward took his skates, and swiftly
  Toward the ice-bound lakelet flew.

Foolish boy! his gentle mother
  Had forbidden him to go;
For she saw the danger lurking
  Under new-formed ice and snow.

Soon the merry skaters, dashing
  O'er the moonlit lake, he sees;
And he hears their glad young voices
  Humming like the busy bees.

All forgotten is his mother,
  And her warning kindly said;
Soon among the bravest skaters
  Loudly shouted truant Ned.

Now he nears a spot, where hidden,
  Is a hole of frightful size;
But the bonfire's dancing brightness
  Dazzles his bewildered eyes.

Down he goes! the icy water
  Filling throat and ears and nose,—
"Ned is drowning! Can't you save him?
  Oh, he's sinking! There he goes!"

See! poor Ned is slowly rising,
  Almost senseless with his fears;
His cold hands are grasped above him,
  And a friendly voice he hears.

Boys now drag him, chilled and dripping,
  Gasping, to the icy shore;
And with stiffened lips he whispers,
  "I'll play truant *nevermore*."

AN AQUARIUM.

Did you ever see one? Many a child has visited the "Aquarial Gardens" in Boston, and looked with delight upon the strange and beautiful inhabitants of the sea, with the pebbles, coral, and shells, that are gathered in glass tanks, of which there is a large number to be examined. Our artist has given you here a fine picture of an aquarium.

A friend of the children sends us a very interesting letter, describing what may be seen near her home, which is on the sea-shore. She gives an account of the coral insects. You will notice in this picture the star-fish, the coral, and other things of which she writes. This is her letter: —

"Come to our bay when the day is pleasant, the water smooth as ice, and when the tide has gone out, leaving the gray rocks and brown seaweed bare; enter our little boat, and I will show you some of these curiosities.

"Let us row across to the lighthouse-pier, which stretches far out. Once a treacherous sand-bank was here, covered with water, and many a vessel struck, when the sailors thought themselves safe in port, till this stone pier and the lighthouse were built over it to warn them of danger. We will row up close, and steady our boat by holding to the bunches of seaweed that grow thickly here, while we look for the coral.

"Here is a cavity left by the falling out of one of the granite stones. Lift up the curtain of seaweed and look in; is it not pretty as a fairy cave? The gray walls are lined with white or red enamel; this, also, is made by insects, but too small for you to see. Here and there is a ball of white or brown jelly, waiting for the tide to open into wavy fringes. These are the *anemones;* and numbers of colored shells are being moved about by their occupants, which are all life and enjoyment among the bright-green seaweed.

"What is that lovely, sparkling blue? Only common brown seaweed when out of the water, but looking as if it had stolen the color of the sky when in it; that we call the *chondrus*, but I must not give you any more hard names to remember.

"Ah! here is the coral. Do you see on that shelf of rock, which the tide has not yet reached, something like a white rose pressed flat, or a cluster of white snow-flakes? Look closer, you will see it is something like the coral to which you have been accustomed; a number of little stars close together, with a tiny dot in the center of each.

"Now let us wait till the tide rises and the water just covers them. Its first touch will waken the little animals now shut so quietly, each in its own cell. Ah! there they come; that largest one has put out a little circle of white fingers, delicate as the finest silk; now another and another, all waving and stretching and moving and reaching about in the water, till even to the tiniest ones on the outside of the cluster, all are full of life. But what are they doing? Eating; their mothers do not cook for them, nor their fathers find food for them, yet the good All-father feeds even these little things, for he cares for all.

"Atoms too small for you to see are swept past them by the water, and their delicate fingers catch them and push them down into their mouths, and so the insects are nourished and make for themselves, each his little cell. What's this! All have disappeared, shut up as closely as if they had never been open. Yet the water goes over them as smoothly as ever. What is the matter?

"Look! Don't you see the great, purple star-fish creeping along with his hundred feet and thousand suckers? The hungry giant fancied he was about to have a good supper, but scarcely has his foremost point touched the coral than all are safely folded away. Creep on, Mr. Star, with those great rays of yours! Walk over the coral; you will find only a hard-edged surface, no tender little morsels to feed on; and then be off, and surprise some unfortunate muscle that has just opened his shell for a drink of clear water!

"Now he is gone, and out pops one little finger, and another, and in less than a minute they are as lively and active as ever. There comes a wave and sweeps a heavy bunch of seaweed over them, but they do not close. They are not so foolish as some little children I have heard of, afraid of every thing they meet; especially, afraid of the dark.

"'But how,' you ask, 'do they know the difference between the starfish and the seaweed?' I can scarcely tell you, except that it is by the use of a certain power which God has given them, and which we call *instinct*, and very quickly and willingly they obey its teachings.

"God has given much higher powers to you, children: reason and knowledge and parents and teachers, to show you what is right and wrong; yet I am afraid you do not always obey these as readily as the poor little coral insects do their only Teacher, though you are in far more danger.

"And now the tide is rising over the mouth of the cave, so we will drop the seaweed curtain, and leave them to their quiet happiness."

"NOT THANKFUL ENOUGH."

I ENTERED the cars at N—— one morning, to go on the Connecticut River Railroad to S——, and sat down beside a little fellow whom, from his appearance, I took for a boy of perhaps nine or ten years. There was something in his countenance which immediately arrested my attention. While an expression of content, and even of peace and joy, rested on his pale face, I could see also the evidences of suffering; and I noticed at the same time, as additional proof that he was subject to some infirmity, a pair of crutches standing by the car-window.

I commenced conversation with him, and found him very intelligent, and quite willing to talk with me. Thus I learned that, instead of being only nine years old, he was fourteen; that at the age of three years he had been injured by a fall, and from that time, now eleven years, he had been a hopeless, suffering cripple. I felt much interested in his case, and greatly benefited by his words, they were so full of meekness and submission; for this dear boy, cut off by his misfortune from all the sports and the out-door amusements in which boys so much delight, expressed, with beaming eyes, his happiness in the love of that Saviour who had seen fit to make his path through so much trial.

When I reminded him that he had no doubt been kept by his lameness from many temptations to wicked ways which he would have met in the streets, "Oh, yes!" he said, "I know that. And then I have a great many blessings, — a great many things to make me happy. I often feel that *I am not thankful enough for them.*"

As I looked down upon that little form, checked in its growth by suffering, and into that white, patient face, and as I heard the expressions of trust in and love for Him who "doth not afflict willingly," my heart smote me for my own ingratitude to my heavenly Father.

Dear children, when the day appointed for "Thanksgiving" comes, do you ever find it hard to tell what you have to thank God for? Does it ever seem to you that the day may be a very good one for grown-up people, — for *men* who have gathered great harvests, or done a large business, or had richly freighted ships come in, while you find it hard to see what little boys and girls have to do with being thankful?

Sit down a moment and think of your blessings. Remember this little lame boy. Remember the deaf and dumb, the blind, and multitudes of other children who are suffering in various ways, and see if you have not *something* to make you thankful; and it may be that you too will be ready to say, "I have many blessings, and I feel that I am not thankful enough for them!"

KATE AND THE GOAT.

LITTLE KATE had many friends, and was generally a cheerful, good-natured child; but she had a great fault, which sometimes got her into trouble,—she was very stubborn. One day she had to cross a stream of water on a plank, which served as a foot bridge; but just as she got on one end, a goat stepped on the other. Now Kate resolved that she would not give up to a goat; so they met on the middle of the plank, and stood still for a few minutes looking at each other. The goat *could not* turn back; so, as Kate *would not*, he ended the dispute by pushing her into the water, and walking quickly over. She soon screamed for help, and was taken out dripping wet, and quite mortified. Though we should be *firm* in matters of duty and principle, let us not be *stubborn* about trifles, nor too proud to yield when we ought to do so.

THE ALPINE PASS.

Do you know, boys, that you have entered upon the most difficult and perilous passage of your life? Ascending from childhood up to manhood is like climbing up the steep, slippery sides of a high mountain, where the way all along abounds in dangerous places, sharp turns, abrupt ascents, fearful precipices, and yawning chasms. Oh, how hard it is to get to the top in safety! How many, many boys fall and are lost for ever!

I rode up the St. Gothard once, among the Alps, and I wish I could describe the journey vividly to you, for I so often think of it when I meet with a boy of your age, and perceive the jeopardy which he is constantly in. The road was a splendid one; there was no fault to find with that. It was originally planned and constructed by Napoleon the Great, and is now kept in the finest order by the government. And *your* road is a good one; there could not be a surer or safer one. If you walk right on and up in the path of truth and duty, all will be well with you. The surroundings, the liabilities, the side-way exposures, are what make it so dangerous.

We started on a bright, sunny morning, just after a deep snow, for it was mid-winter; and a large party of men had been sent ahead to shovel the path and clear the way for us; just as your parents and teachers have, as it were, been sent before you, that by their experience your way might be made smoother and more secure. It will be well for you to listen to their counsels and heed their suggestions. As we could not go in the usual conveyance,—the great lumbering diligence,—the whole company of travellers could not proceed together; so we had to divide into pairs, and filled a line of twenty-five single sleighs, or rather rude sledges on low runners. In these narrow vehicles the two passengers sat facing each other, and the driver in front. These drivers, or pilots I might call them, are very expert and careful men, thoroughly acquainted with the way, and ever on the alert to perceive and avoid danger. They directed us to dress very snugly, not allowing a vail, cape, or scarf to be worn, unless it was fastened down closely, and not suffering us to place in the sleigh an umbrella, cane, or any thing that would project. Why? Because the winds sweep in sudden and fierce gusts down those hights, and around those sharp angles in the road, might catch in some fluttering garment, and, filling it like a sail, whirl us in a moment over the awful precipice; or a projecting article from the sledge might strike against the rock in going rapidly around the curve, and upset our frail conveyance, and topple us down the abyss to a horrible death. The road wound up and around the sides of the mountain in zigzag lines cut into the rock like shelves. As our sleigh was almost the last of the long procession, I could look up and see a line of a dozen or twenty on a narrow ledge, almost perpendicularly over my head, driving along at a furious rate, and in a moment or two we were whirled up a steep place and around a point, and were there ourselves, the others still higher on. In many places, I could put out one hand and touch the rock that rose like a solid wall straight up to an immense distance beside me, and. turning my head on the other side, could look down, down, hundreds and thousands of feet into the most terrific gulfs.

"Don't look down there," said the driver; "it will make you faint and dizzy, and you may fall out."

"Do accidents often occur on these mountain passes?" we asked.

"Not very often," he said, "for we understand our business pretty well. I've driven up and down the St. Gothard almost every day for twenty-five years, and our horses are well trained, too. But sometimes something gives way, or the animals take fright, and then nothing can stop them. In a team of six horses, if one goes wrong, all the rest will go too. A diligence went over, just about in this spot, last summer."

We shuddered to think of the horrid catastrophe.

Now, dear boys, don't you see some points of resemblance between this fearful mountain-ascent, and the way in which you must go?

You have a cautious, wise Pilot, who never errs,—Jesus. If you will but follow his directions, you will be safe.

You must dress for your journey; that is, clothe yourselves around snugly with correct principles, good habits, and firm resolutions. Bad habits will be the fluttering, projecting things that will catch the evil wind, and be the occasion of your overthrow. So be sure to leave them all behind, or put them under your feet.

Don't go too near the edge of the precipice, curious to look over the rugged sides, lest you should lose your balance and fall. Keep your eyes straight forward, "looking unto Jesus," and never turn to the right hand or to the left. Don't stop on those dizzy hights to gather flowers, or heed the enticing voices of gay, careless companions. Follow your Leader closely; obey him, and you will find yourself, by and by, safely arrived on the sublime hights of a noble and virtuous manhod.

Happy, thrice happy are those who make the perilous ascent from the sunny vales of infancy, through the slippery paths of youth, up to mature age, uninjured by accident or stain of sin.

TIDY LEARNING TO READ.

Tidy was a little slave at the South. She had to wait upon two young girls, Amelia and Susie, the children of her master, and every day she was accustomed to walk to the school-house with them, to carry their books and the basket which contained their dinner. But she always left them at the door. The school was not for *her*.

One summer's morning they were earlier than usual, and emerging from the woods, warm and weary with their long walk, they threw themselves down upon the rock over which, in the early day, the shadow of the trees refreshingly fell. Amelia turned her face toward the run, and, lulled by the gentle murmuring of the water and the humming of the insects, was soon quietly asleep; Susie, with an apronful of burs, was making furniture for the play-house which they were arranging in a cleft of the rock; and Tidy, who carried the books, was busily turning over the leaves and amusing herself with the pictures.

"My sakes!" she exclaimed presently, "what a funny cretur! See that great lump on his back!" and she pointed with her finger to the picture of a camel. "Miss Susie! what *is* that? Is it a lame horse?"

"Why, no, Tidy; that's a camel; 'tisn't a horse at all. I was reading that very place yesterday,—let me see;" and, taking the book, she read very intelligently a brief account of the wonderful animal.

"How queer!" said Tidy, deeply interested. "And is there something in this book about all the pictures?"

"Yes," answered Susie; "if you could only read now, you would know about every one. See here, on the next page is an elephant; see his great tusks, and his monstrous long trunk;" and the child read to her attentive listener of another of the wonders of creation.

"How I wish *I* could read; why can't I?" asked Tidy; and the little colored face was turned up, full of animation. "I don't b'lieve but I could learn as well as you."

"Why, of course you could," answered Amelia, who had risen quite refreshed by her short nap. "I don't see why not. You can't go to school, you know, because mother wants you to work; but *I* could teach you just as well as not."

"Oh, could you?—will you? Do begin!" cried the eager child. "Oh, Miss Mely, if you only would, I'd do any thing for you."

"Look here," said Amelia, seizing the book from her sister's hands, and by virtue of superior age constituting herself the teacher; "do you see those lines?" and she pointed to the columns of letters on the first page.

"Yes," said the ready pupil, all attention.

"Well, those are letters; the alphabet, they call it. Every one of them has got a name, and when you have learned to know them all perfectly, so that you can call them all right, wherever you see 'em, why, then you can read any thing."

"Any thing?" asked Tidy, in amazement.

"Yes, any thing; all kinds of books and papers, and the Bible, and every thing."

"I can learn *them*, I'se sure I can," said Tidy. "Let's begin now."

"Well, you see that first one,—that's A. You see how it's made; two lines go right up to a point, and then a straight one across. Now say, what is it?"

"A."

"Yes; and now the next one,—that's B. There's a straight line down and two curves on the front. What's that?"

"B."

"Now you must remember those two. I shan't tell you any more this morning, and I shall make you do just as Miss Agnes used to make me. Miss Agnes was our governess at home before we came here to school. She made me take a newspaper—see, here's a piece—and prick the letters on it with a pin. Now you take this piece of paper and prick every A and every B that you can find on it, and to-morrow I'll show you some more."

Just then the bell sounded from the school-house, and Amelia and Susan went to their duties, but not with half so glad a heart as Tidy set herself to hers.

Thus Tidy began to learn to read. She had very many and very great difficulties to struggle against, but she persevered and was at last successful. As the years passed by, and she was enabled, by Him who watches over the lowly, to understand what she read, the hymns she loved and the

Word of God were made the means of leading her to Jesus Christ.

Tidy at length obtained her freedom, and she still lives, a happy Christian. Though poor, she can say with a glad heart, "I have every thing I want, for God is my Father. He gives me every thing he sees best for me."

"STINGINESS."

"Give to him that asketh thee, and from him that would borrow of thee, turn not thou away."

"Lizzie, won't you lend me your new lead-pencil to finish drawing my horse with,—mine is worn so short and stumpy?"

Little Georgie looked up pleadingly from his seat on the floor, where he was bending over a rough drawing in an old blank-book.

"No, George, I can't," answered his sister, a little pettishly; "I'm afraid you'll break off the point."

"No; I'll be very careful; please lend it to me, Lizzie?"

"I can't, I say; don't ask me again."

"Why not, Lizzie?" asked her grown-up cousin, Grace, who was sitting by the window, busy with some embroidery; "suppose he does break off the point, you can sharpen it again; or, if you can not do it nicely, I will do it for you; don't be disobliging."

"Oh, well, I don't like to lend my things, Cousin Grace. They always get spoiled in some way. Maybe he'll break off the ivory head, or scratch it, or something, and I want to keep it all nice and new."

Cousin Grace made no answer to this short and selfish speech.

"I will lend you mine, Georgie," she said; "it is away up stairs, but no matter." And she rose and laid aside her thimble and scissors and work.

Georgie looked up with a delighted "Thank you," and Lizzie pouted, but she did not offer to save her cousin the trouble; so the kind young lady went up stairs and brought down her own pencil for the little boy, who was made happy for an hour, by the nice, bold strokes with which he could now shade off the horse he was drawing.

The next morning, as Cousin Grace was again seated near the window, embroidering, Lizzie came up to her and said,—

"Won't you be so kind as to lend me your small scissors, Cousin Grace? Mine are so blunt they won't cut nice eyelets at all,—and I shall spoil this band."

"No, Lizzie, I can't," said Cousin Grace, mimicking exactly the tone in which Lizzie had answered her little brother the day before. "I'm afraid you might break off the points."

"Why, no, I shan't," said Lizzie, scarcely knowing whether her cousin was in earnest or not; "I'm not going to cut tow cloth with them."

"Well you might tarnish their brightness, or dull them, or something," answered Cousin Grace, in a sort of pettish drawl; "I like to keep my things nice and new."

Lizzie could not mistake her meaning now. She turned very red, and, walking away without a word, sat down, and went on hacking away with her blunt scissors in silence. Cousin Grace sewed on silently, too, for some time; but she was very kind-hearted, and could not bear to punish her little cousin very long. So she said, presently, in a kind, grave tone,—

"I suppose you think me a little hard in denying you so small a favor, do you, Lizzie?"

Lizzie blushed again, but did not speak. She knew it was only just.

"I am sorry to say that I have seen this fault growing upon you, my dear child," Cousin Grace continued, "and it is a grievous one, and makes the person guilty of it disagreeable to every one else. How can Georgie love you, when you refuse all his little requests, and never put yourself out to make him happy? Or how can the rest of us love you when we see you so disobliging? And more than that, God is displeased to see you so selfish. Did you know that you were breaking a command of his yesterday, when you refused to lend Georgie your pencil? He says, 'Give to him that asketh thee, and from him that would borrow of thee, turn not thou away.'"

"But I have heard mother say that it was not right to borrow," said Lizzie, a little sullenly.

"And so it is not right to make a habit of borrowing. It is a very bad plan for neighbors to be constantly borrowing among each other; they should try to have what is necessary, of their own, and do without what they can not get for themselves. But that rule does not apply to such little acts of kindness and courtesy. Christ gave this command, as he did many others, to teach us to be unselfish, and care for the pleasure of others as much as for our own. I want you to learn that text, Lizzie, and promise me that you will try to act according to its spirit, hereafter. And, now, here are the scissors."

So Lizzie came to get them, and kissed her Cousin Grace, and promised to remember what had been said to her.

THE "GROTTO DEL CANE."

There is a cavern near Naples, in Italy, called the "Grotto of the Dog," because, while people who walk through it erect are unharmed, the dogs, running with their noses to the ground, drop suddenly dead a few steps within.

There is a very poisonous gas that men and animals throw off from their lungs while breathing. It is called "carbonic acid gas," and is the same as that which comes from burning charcoal, and it kills people who are shut up in a close room with it, and can not get the pure air. There is a great deal of this gas in dark places, pits, and sewers, and underground sinks, and the workmen who go down into them often lose their lives.

It is this sort of gas that lies at the bottom of the "Grotto del Cane," and takes away the breath of many a poor dog. I suppose you would like to know why God made this poisonous acid, that is so fatal to those who come in contact with it. I will tell you something about the air we breathe, and try to make it so simple that you will understand, and see the wisdom of the great Creator, who doeth all things well.

I went to hear some very pleasant lectures on this subject not long since. They were given for children, and I like to be taught as the little people are, so I found myself among them.

The professor told us that the air is composed of two gases. You know a gas is something you can not see or take hold of, though it touches you all the time.

One of these gases is called oxygen, and without it you could not live. The other is called nitrogen, and is, by itself, a very bad, ugly gas, and would destroy your life in a room where it is.

Then the lecturer took a jar of the oxygen and thrust a lighted taper into it, and it burned brighter, but when he thrust it into a jar of nitrogen, out it went in a trice.

"You see, good young people," said he, "what a great difference there is in the two gases; which do you like best?"

Of course they all said, "Oxygen." "And yet," continued he, "God has given us only one-fifth of oxygen in the common air, to four-fifths of nitrogen. Would you like to know why?"

"Yes, sir! yes, sir!" cried the many voices.

"I will tell you what this pure oxygen would do if you were to breathe it alone," said he. "It would make your pulse beat faster and faster, and swell your veins almost to bursting, and you would be frisking about in a wilder and wilder mood, until at last you would be quite frantic, and would die. It is too stimulating for us; that is the reason why God has diluted or weakened it with so much of this nitrogen, which by itself is so bad a gas."

"What if we were to have the nitrogen only?" asked an intelligent little boy, who was an attentive listener.

"Why, your breath would cease in a minute, or at least as quick as you had used up what oxygen there was in your lungs when you were shut up. But I want to tell you something else that I think very wonderful indeed," said the professor, "about the carbonic acid gas that you and I, and all the people in this room, are throwing off. Let me see. There are four hundred people, and if we remain two hours, we shall throw off from our lungs enough of this gas to make twenty-five pounds of charcoal."

The children began to look about to see if the windows were let down.

"That is right," said the lecturer; "we must have some way for this poison to escape. Do any of you feel dull or drowsy?"

"My head aches," said a little girl in the corner, where it was close and dark, and the children were packed tightly.

"What gas do we need here, children, to purify the air?" asked the professor.

"Oxygen," was the ready answer.

"Well, where shall we get it?"

"Open the windows; let in more good air," said the little people.

"That is true. Perhaps you have heard the dreadful fate of the poor creatures that were put in the hold of a ship during a storm, and the hatches closed upon them. When the hatches were reopened, there were crowds of dead and dying, all from the effect of this carbonic acid gas that so many lungs were throwing off, while no fresh supply of oxygen could be obtained."

Some of the children had heard it, and all said, "How dreadful!"

"Would you believe that this carbonic acid gas, that is such certain death to the animal creation, can be necessary to the life of any thing?"

"No," said the little voices, "no, no!"

"But it is; — the plants give us oxygen and take to themselves this that we discard, and it nourishes them and makes them beautiful, even as the oxygen fills us with vigor and life."

It needs the light to help the plants in their good work, and all the day the blessed sun is doing its part with the plants to keep the air right for us.

"Isn't it strange," said the professor, "that we and the plants are so dependent upon each other? You must never despise even what you may call a worthless weed, dear children, but remember that it is giving you that beautiful oxygen that is so necessary to your life, and taking for its own use that ugly carbonic gas, that would be so fatal to the animal system if it were allowed to accumulate all over the earth, as it does in the dark, unsunned places.

"There is something I want the boys and girls to learn from this 'Grotto del Cane,'" pursued the professor, "and that is, if our moral nature, our souls, will but go through this life erect, they will breathe a pure, sweet atmosphere, and be unharmed by the poisonous stratum that lurks at their feet; but if they grovel to the level of a sinful world, if they go nosing about like a dog, instead of lifting themselves up like men, they will be sure not only to get all the bad, lower, vicious air, but will sink down into a sudden and dreadful death. But perhaps I am not making the lesson plain to you; I see some of you yawning as if you had no interest in what I am saying."

The children brightened up a little, and seemed earnest again.

The professor turned to a lad who sat near him on a side-bench. "My son," said he, "did you ever get into a group of bad men, who were drunken and swearing?"

"Yes, sir," answered the lad.

"It is a more poisonous air than carbonic acid gas makes, if one stops to breathe it, isn't it, children?"

"Yes! yes!" cried a hundred voices.

"Why?—does it kill any *body?*"

The children caught at the emphasis upon the word *body.*

"It kills the *soul,*" said they.

"That is true," said the professor; "and how are we to keep from harm?"

"By lifting our souls up to God in prayer, and walking straight through, instead of stopping to listen, and by and by getting down to the same level of wickedness," said the lecturer, as the young people looked to him for instruction.

"Let me hope that all the boys and girls whose faces are before me to-day will so pass through all trials and temptations that no harm shall happen to their immortal souls."

TOO MUCH TROUBLE.

"I HAVE wished I was a Christian a good many times," said Harry to his mother, as he laid down his paper. "I should be one if there were not so many things to do. I never could do them all. I have tried a good many times."

"What is there to do, my son, but to give up what is wrong, and do what is right? You wish to do that?"

"Yes, mother, but that is what I can not do. It is too much trouble."

"It was not too much trouble for the Saviour to leave heaven, suffer, and die for you," said his mother.

"I know I ought to please him," said Harry, with eyes fixed on the floor. "But I am doing wrong all the while. I pray, and that does not stop me."

"Your heart is wrong, my dear child. It loves sin. You can never love God till your heart is washed in the blood of Christ. Pray for a new heart. Then you will delight in doing God's will. If you keep praying, he will answer and bless you."

www.ingramcontent.com/pod-product-compliance
Lightning Source LLC
LaVergne TN
LVHW021411110826
845150LV00007B/1877

* 9 7 8 1 4 2 5 5 1 1 5 9 3 *